IMAGES
of Wales

CARDIFF RUGBY FOOTBALL CLUB
1876-1939

The South Stand of the Cardiff ground in the early 1900s. The area of land behind the trees became the site of the Cardiff General Post Office.

IMAGES
of Wales

CARDIFF RUGBY FOOTBALL CLUB 1876-1939

Compiled by
Duncan Gardiner and Alan Evans

TEMPUS

First published 1999
Copyright © Duncan Gardiner and Alan Evans, 1999

Tempus Publishing Limited
The Mill, Brimscombe Port,
Stroud, Gloucestershire, GL5 2QG

ISBN 0 7524 1608 1

Typesetting and origination by
Tempus Publishing Limited
Printed in Great Britain by
Midway Clark Printing, Wiltshire

A selection of present and forthcoming titles from Tempus Publishing:

Cardiff City Football Club 1899-1947
Cardiff City Football Club 1947-71
CARDIFF RUGBY CLUB 1939-99
Glamorgan County Cricket Club I
Glamorgan County Cricket Club II
Llanelli Rugby Club
Newport County FC
Newport Rugby Club 1875-1950
Newport Rugby Club 1950-2000
Swansea Town Football Club 1912-64

Please contact us for a full stocklist.

Contents

Acknowledgements

No book of this nature could be produced without ready assistance from a myriad sources and we have been extremely fortunate in the number of people who have willingly given up their time and granted access to personal collections, much of which has never been published in a book before.

Thanks must go to Gareth Davies (the chief executive of Cardiff Rugby Football Club plc) and his board of directors for permission to use material from the club's trophy room. To Ifor Davies of Print Partnership and Ken Poole, for unveiling his unique collection of memorabilia, we give special thanks.

This in no way dilutes our gratitude also to: Tim Auty, John Billot, Harry and Jackie Bowcott, Alan Brinkworth, Sarah Bruntlett, Carrie Culverwell, Anne Davies, John (St Athan) Davies, Howard Evans, John M. Jenkins, Colin Howe, Richard Hudson, Ken Jarrett, John M. Jenkins, Tony Lewis, Jack Matthews, the Musee d'Art Moderne de la Ville Paris, Bill and Dennis O'Neill, Brian Powell, Dave Richards, Noel Upfold, Bleddyn Williams and Enid Wooller for their invaluable contributions.

Finally, we thank Tempus Publishing for setting a frequently frustrating but forever fascinating task of discovering more about a club (and a sport) that intrigues and enthralls us.

Duncan Gardiner and Alan Evans
Cardiff 1999

Introduction

It was difficult to believe, even as the new Millennium Stadium was rising in the very heart of Cardiff, the capital of Wales, that rugby followers will ever call it by that title. For close to 125 years, the world of sport has known the home of rugby football in the city as the Arms Park and that is surely how it will be referred to in the future.

The name is also inextricably associated with Cardiff Rugby Football Club and the rise in majesty and importance of the club and the ground are essentially linked – through players, events, visiting teams and, eventually (and notwithstanding some neighbourly wars), the very proximity with the national team and the Welsh Rugby Union itself.

This book not only explores many of the great names and games that have graced the Arms Park but tells also a story of romance and routine, of success and sorrow, of triumphs and tragedies. Sadly, rugby football was initially not well covered in photographic terms but, in travelling pictorially through the history of Cardiff Rugby Club from its formation in 1876 up to the outbreak of the Second World War, the reader will find pictures and images hitherto unpublished, as well as new facts and anecdotes about some of the personalities who have contributed to making the club a name known throughout the world by playing a crucial role in the evolution of rugby football.

From the days when the burgeoning importance of Cardiff was reflected in the business of the Cardiff Arms (the hotel whose land gave the ground its name) to the years when Cardiff took on, and beat, in quick succession, most of the world's best, through golden ages and relatively fallow years, the fascinating story of a leading club emerges, via its characters and personalities – both on and off the field. Some famous names and incidents may well have slipped through the photographic net but the club history is festooned with such men and matches.

Nor is this merely a man's book about what was considered to be primarily a man's game. The 'fur-coat brigade' may today be a phrase of contempt aimed at those ladies (accompanying the 'suits' in the corporate hospitality rooms) who know nothing of the sport but only about the social benefits of being able to say, in the words of Max Boyce, that 'I was there', but, as you will see, there has been a history of female followers of Cardiff. This following continues to have repercussions today, nearly ninety years later, as members of those families still support the club. Indeed, family involvement has always been a notable element of the Cardiff club, with several brothers contributing huge efforts as well as fathers and sons. Many of these families have helped in the compilation of this book through their own personal photographs, programmes and scrapbooks.

The essence, then, of a local club formed through the amalgamation of two others to play on the Arms Park is a vital part of the story. However, it was through the exposure of the club, both at home and abroad to the famous rugby nations, that its real reputation was gained and the memorabilia from these historic meetings helps to recreate these achievements.

For the rugby historian and the connoisseur there are many fascinating photographs and prints but, for the more casual and possibly socially aware individual, there are also details of interest: whether it be the low amount of the peppercorn rent being asked by the Marquess of Bute's family for the use of the land in front of the Cardiff Arms, the meals eaten at sumptuous banquets after famous matches, the price of admission and season tickets, or the protests of members at the amounts of money being paid for continental visits (costs that look bizarrely small today).

It is because of one of those trips to France that the Cardiff club – *L'Equipe de Cardiff* – became important even in the world of modern art. This is just one of the stories told in this evocative and, in many ways, unique book about an important piece in the jigsaw of an important city. Undoubtedly there are other important images of Cardiff rugby out there – forgotten or undiscovered in attics or in bottom drawers, in photographic albums, in scrapbooks or on walls. The authors of this book would be delighted to hear of any such items which will help to contribute towards a total recall of rugby football.

In the meantime, simply turn back the clock and enjoy some images from the past in the remarkable history of Cardiff Rugby Football Club.

One
From the Cardiff Arms to the Arms Park

After members of Cardiff Wanderers and Glamorgan Football Club had decided, in September 1876, to merge and become Cardiff Football Club, the committee chose black with white skull and crossbones as their colours and were known briefly as The Pirates until parents objected to their sons wearing such emblems. At the end of the first season, they changed to blue and black stripes after they had seen such a kit being worn by T.W. Rees, a Cambridge student who played for Cardiff.

The military made use of the land in front of the Cardiff Arms Hotel, which was to become the Arms Park, in the days before rugby arrived there (in 1871). *Above*: The band of the Royal Glamorgan Militia and the regiment itself are drawn up. *Below*: A detachment of the Royal Glamorgan Infantry go on parade.

The Cardiff Arms Hotel, which was demolished in 1882, was the coaching inn whose name became irrevocably linked world-wide with the Cardiff club and Welsh rugby. The inn had grown in importance with the evolution of travel and, later, with the commercial development of Cardiff as it became the greatest coal port in the world.

The rear of the Cardiff Arms backed on to what is now Castle Street.

Views from Cardiff Castle in the 1880s, after the River Taff had been diverted by the Second Marquess of Bute to assist the city's growth between 1848 and 1853. These images show the land by the Cardiff Arms Hotel looking south down what today is Westgate Street and west across Cardiff Bridge. Various sporting events took place on the land now occupied by the Millennium Stadium and the Cardiff Arms Park. In 1875 (the year before the formation of Cardiff RFC), for example, at a sports meeting, an extraordinary drop-kick of 145 yards by a man named Lukes was recorded. The riverside meadow had become the headquarters of Cardiff Cricket Club and, on the formation of Cardiff RFC, the first practice match was played, on 14 October 1878, on the Park in front of the cricket pavilion. Both cricket and football clubs were charged a mere shilling-a-year peppercorn rent by the Third Marquess of Bute and his successor.

The Cardiff club's first captain was T.S. Donaldson Selby, who had been captain of Glamorgan and whose new side played three matches in that opening season of 1876/77, losing at Newport but beating Swansea and Merthyr at home. Newport and Swansea had previously been able to beat the two original clubs separately, a fact which led to a move for amalgamation.

By the 1878/79 season, the fixture list had grown to twenty matches. Cardiff won sixteen and reached the final of the South Wales Challenge Cup, only to lose comfortably to Newport. The side that met Newport at Sophia Gardens, because the Arms Park was not yet able to accommodate the expected crowd, that March day in 1879 before about 4,000 people (despite gate money of sixpence being controversially charged – the gate receipts were £72) was, from left to right, back row: W.G. Jones (Umpire), A.W. Watts, P.K. Heard, A.J. Evans. Second row: ? Fleming, S. Thomas, S. Thomas, B.E. Girling, R.H. Foa (Captain), T.W. Rees, W.D. Phillips, J.A. Jones. Front row: B. Godfrey, E.D. Thomas, Read McDonald, W.B. Ferries, Fred Perch, B.B. Mann.

W.D. Phillips (above left) and B.E. Girling (above right), were two of the three Cardiff players in Wales's first international match against England on 19 February 1881, when, on Mr Richardson's field at Blackheath, the Welsh were routed by 8 goals and 5 tries to nil. Some things never change: the heavy score led to criticism that the selectors had been biased and, without one player from either Swansea or Llanelli, there may have been truth in the suggestion. W.D. Phillips, in fact, was either captain or vice-captain for Cardiff's first nine seasons, having previously captained the Wanderers, before becoming club president and also a member of the International Board, while Girling skippered the team in 1881/82.

B.B. Mann (left), who had been a registered member of the club since its second season when the fee was 2s 6d, was the third Cardiff player in that first international, three weeks after which the first Welsh Football Union (the Welsh Rugby Union of today) was founded. Mann was vice-captain of Cardiff in 1881/82. All three of these players were forwards.

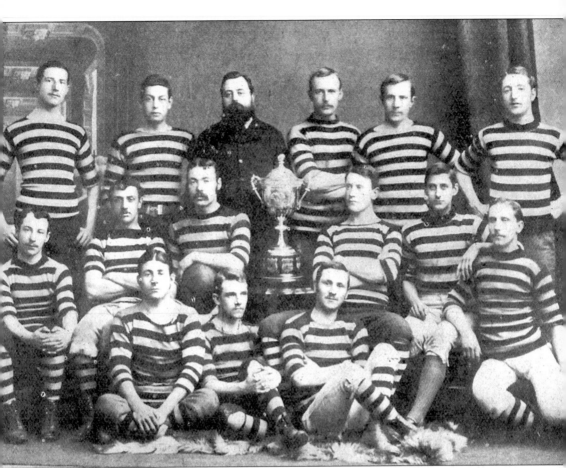

The Cardiff team with the South Wales Challenge Trophy, having beaten Llanelly (as it was then spelt) on 12 March 1881. The side was, from left to right, back row: J.A. Jones, J.S. Smith, H. Shrewbrooke (Umpire), B.B. Mann, Tom Williams, W.H. Treatt. Middle row: W.B. Norton, P.K. Heard, W.D. Phillips, C.H. Sewell, Vipond Davies, A.H. Hybart. Front row: E.D. Thomas, R. Trotter, A.J. Evans. After beating Newport and Pontypridd to reach the final, there was no score at the end of normal time against Llanelly and an extra ten minutes each way was played. Four minutes from the end of the second period, P.K. Heard scored a try which was so disputed that Mitchell, a Llanelly player, refused to give up the ball for the conversion and Cardiff were adjudged the winners. In the earlier round, after winning at Newport, Cardiff's players were reported to have been jostled, kicked and beaten by 'a crowd of ruffians'.

By the 1884/85 season, Cardiff's playing strength had grown to the extent that, while the First XV had twenty-four matches (of which they won fifteen), the Second XV, under the captaincy of Cholton Jones, played eighteen games – and were unbeaten. Nor was that all, they were delighted also to beat the Firsts by a drop goal and a try to nil, with the date – 1 April – having nothing to do with it. The invincible Seconds were, from left to right, back row: Lionel Taylor, H. James, E. Emery, J.A. Sant, S.D. Evans, R.T. Duncan, W.R. Rees, A.J. Halsey, G. Wensley, A.F. Bland, A.J. Hybart, F.I. James and Q.D. Kedzlie. Seated: J.B. Coe, W.E. Jarman, W.M. Douglas, Cholton Jones (Captain), O.J. Evans, D.E. Jones and J.D. Evans (Umpire).

Left: Dan E. Jones, captain of the Second XV in 1885/86, when they were unbeaten for the second year running, went on to lead the team for six consecutive seasons. During their second invincible season they scored 22 goals and 44 tries, conceding only 1 goal and 3 tries. *Right:* W.M. 'Billy' Douglas, who joined Cardiff in 1881/82, served as player and administrator on and off for more than fifty years, until 1940. He won 4 Welsh caps, captained Cardiff in 1886/87 and, the previous season, had scored 4 tries in a match against Newport.

Two
The Creative Years

Frank and Philip Hancock, two of three brothers from Wiveliscombe in Somerset who made their mark in Cardiff both in rugby and through the family brewery. While Philip (right) also played for Blackheath and was capped 3 times by England, Frank (left) captained Cardiff in 1885/86 when they lost only one of twenty-seven matches – to Moseley on the last day of the season at the Arms Park – and was also responsible for bringing the four-man three-quarter line to rugby during 1883/84. Cardiff, short of a back, had selected him to meet a strong Cheltenham College side and he played so well that they were reluctant to drop him for the following game and opted for an extra three-quarter. Before this, rugby had been chiefly for the forwards and the four three-quarter system was not adopted by the Welsh Rugby Union until 1888/89 and by other home unions in 1893/94. Hancock's dedication to a running game is vividly illustrated by the fact that, in the season of his captaincy, Cardiff neither dropped a goal nor kicked a penalty but scored only tries – 131 of them in fact, with only 4 against.

The first major grandstand to be built at the Arms Park – at a cost of £362. It was opened on Boxing Day 1885, when Frank Hancock's Cardiff side beat Liverpool 15-0. There had been a smaller stand on the sixpenny side (admission charges were now being made at the Arms Park) built in 1881 at a cost of £50 to seat 300 'for the convenience of the spectators and the ladies in particular' and the playing area levelled and re-turfed. With the new stand in 1885 came other improvements before, in 1886/87, another temporary stand was built to 'accommodate the ever-increasing number of spectators'. By then, Cardiff were attracting several thousand and the gate receipts were a magnificent £545 5s 9d, with members' subscriptions of £51 8s 4d. The structures continue to fascinate, as is shown in Alan Brinkworth's 1997 painting (below) which depicts the photograph (above) being taken.

The 1888/89 season saw the first overseas side visit Cardiff when the Maoris, as the first New Zealand team was called, played at the Arms Park on Boxing Day, 1888. The Cardiff team for that season was, from left to right, back row:
A. Duncan (Umpire), W.T. Morgan, W. Ropner, C.S. Arthur, Fred N. Jones, R.T. Duncan, H. Hughes. W.E.O. Williams. Seated: W.E. Jarman, Norman Biggs, S.H. Nicholls, A.F. Hill (Captain), A.F. Bland, A.M. Hill. On the ground:
G. Rosser Evans, Q.D. Kedzlie and J. Mahoney. W.T. Morgan was to become president of the Football Club and, in 1920/21, the first president of the Cardiff Athletic Club, an office he retained until he died in September 1939.

CARDIFF ATHLETIC CLUB

SEASON 1923–4

Lady's Admission Ticket

(NOT TRANSFERABLE)

TO SEASON TICKET HOLDERS' STAND

RESERVED BUT NOT NUMBERED

12/6 INCLUSIVE OF TAX

Ticket No. 293

P.T.O.

Cardiff Football Club

Lady's Ticket

Season 1905-6

CHAS. S. ARTHUR
SECRETARY

By the mid-1880s, spectator interest had increased, with a large number of females becoming involved: one contemporary match report refers to 'an extraordinary number of ladies'. This trend was to grow (see the photographs on pages 62 and 63) and these ladies' membership tickets in the club's trophy room illustrate the enthusiasm. By the end of the 1890/91 season, the club had 663 members and had sold 209 ground tickets and 968 'workmen's' tickets, which had been issued for the first time. New temporary stands had been built at a cost of £254 5s, £142 10s of which was spent on a temporary stand at the Canton end. Other moves included the hiring of a room for training purposes on two nights a week in the Cattle Market Hotel in Quay Street (known simply as the Market Tavern and which, in 1906, was to become the City Arms), which is still frequented by Cardiff followers to this day. In 1892, the club also spent £20 on gymnasium facilities in Stacey Road, Roath, but 'most of the players found it too much trouble to attend' – training was never all that popular!

T.W. Pearson, who scored 128 tries in 180 appearances for the club between 1889 and 1895, was one of the great wing three-quarters of his age. Born in Bombay, he came to England when he was five and was educated at Mill Hill, where he created a sensation by kicking 17 goals in a match against Bedford School. Settling in Cardiff at the age of seventeen in 1889, he captained the side in the 1892/93 season, during which he scored 40 tries, a record which was to stand until beaten by Bleddyn Williams in 1947/48. Later, Pearson moved to Newport to become an engineer and was to add 4 further Welsh caps to the 9 he had won with Cardiff, which included a match as national captain.

C.S. Arthur won 3 caps for Wales and was a great figure in the first fifty years of Cardiff Rugby Club. He played 163 games from 1883, was vice-captain in 1888/89, captain the following season and, perhaps most importantly, secretary from 1882 until his death in December 1926. In 1907, he produced his impressive book *Cardiff RFC: History and Statistics 1876-1906*, which is not only an essential reference work on the early years but also one of the most collectable and valuable additions to any serious rugby library. Charley Arthur is depicted here on two Baines' cards.

Another from the series of shield-shaped cards of John Baines of Bradford, which were produced between the 1880s and 1920s, shows W.E. Jarman, who played eleven seasons for Cardiff. No one is sure how many of these cards actually appeared, but they covered football whether soccer, rugby union or league, and cricket, were sold in packets of six at a halfpenny each by tobacconists, stationers and confectioners and were very popular with schoolboys. The fifty boys with the best assortments of cards each week could redeem them for a free jersey, allowing the cards to be resold at a halfpenny per pack. As many of the cards also carried advertisements on the back – Pears' Soap was a typical example – one way or another they were a huge money-spinner for Mr Baines. The colourful reproductions make them very attractive to collectors today and consequently they are hard to find, with each card worth up to £20.

T.W. Pearson's team of 1892/93 was, from left to right, back row: W.M. Shepherd (Umpire), D. Fitzgerald, A.F. Bland, A.F. Hill, S. Cravos, E.P. Biggs, W. Cope, A. Lewis, C.S. Arthur (by then secretary of the club). Seated: W. Davies, N. Biggs, T.W. Pearson (Captain), J. Elliott, R. Davies. Ground: J. Spavin, D.W. Evans, R.B. Sweet-Escott, S. Biggs and J. Burke. D.W. Evans had, in fact, captained the side the previous season, during which he was injured several times and played in only nineteen of the thirty-one matches. Since his days at Oxford, where he won a blue, he played 117 times for Cardiff, collected 5 Welsh caps and, after his retirement from the game, was to be knighted for his services to the city.

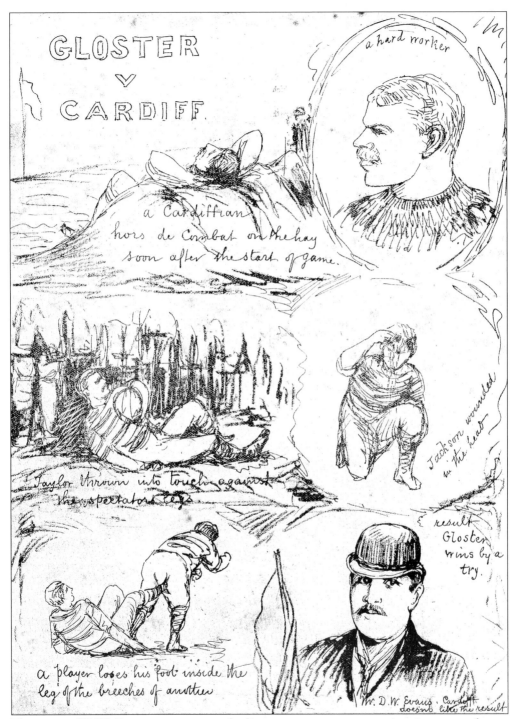

The name of D.W. Evans, now running the line, was to crop up yet again – in cartoon form – during that 1892 season, when the Gloucestershire Magpie clearly had a jaundiced view of a match, even when Gloucester had won.

Six Biggs brothers played for Cardiff between 1886 and 1907. Geoffrey was a lieutenant in the Army and played only the one game for the club in 1906 (against the Barbarians), but J.J.E. Biggs made 18 appearances and E.P Biggs played 57 times while Norman (above left) won 6 Welsh caps and captained his club. Cecil (above right), a centre, had 173 first team games and was regarded as one of the greatest uncapped Welsh players. J.J.E Biggs later became Lord Mayor of Cardiff.

For A.F. Hill, who succeeded Norman Biggs as captain, it was a remarkable second time around as he had previously led the side in 1888/89. Said at the time to have been the best forward to have played for Cardiff – he captained Wales 4 times in his 14 international appearances – he played for the club 153 times between 1883 and 1895.

Selwyn Biggs was the youngest regular playing member of the family to represent Cardiff and was arguably the best. Apart from scoring 46 tries in his 176 appearances, during which he made a splendid half-back pairing with R.B. Sweet-Escott, he was capped 9 times by Wales and captained the club in season 1897/98 – the best since Hancock's year, with only three defeats in thirty-one matches and during the course of which Cardiff beat Newport four times.

The Cardiff team of 1894/95 did not have the best of seasons, winning twenty-one and drawing two of the thirty matches played, but it was an eventful time. The team shown is, from left to right, back row: T. Dobson, J. Elliott, W. Elsey, W. Phillips, A. Lewis, F. Mills, A. Morgan, A.F. Hill (that season's captain but injured here). Seated: W. Davies, T.W. Pearson, R.B. Sweet-Escott, S. Cravos, W. Emery, N. Biggs, and S. Biggs, with T.J. Thomas on the ground. From Christmas onwards, Gwyn Nicholls (see pages 34 and 35) appeared as a regular three-quarter while, sadly, one of the regular forwards, R. Davies, was to lose his life while skating on a pond opposite Hancock's Brewery in Penarth Road.

R.B. (Ralph) Sweet-Escott was one of three brothers who played for Cardiff, but was by far the most successful as he earned 3 Welsh caps, played 148 First XV matches and captained the side.

Cardiff were beaten by Blackheath the following season, to the delight of a contemporary cartoonist in London – but they were not to lose again for another thirty-four matches between the clubs.

H.B. Winfield captained Cardiff for two seasons between 1901 and 1903 and was one of the greatest of the club's full-backs, making 244 appearances for his club and being capped 15 times by Wales. He played for both Cardiff and Wales against the 1905 All Blacks and also captained his country against Ireland in 1908. 'Bert' Winfield's brother, Walter, was captain of the Athletic team in 1901/02 and occasionally stood in for him as full-back. The names of (Gwyn) Nicholls and Winfield then became familiar around the city on the sides of laundry vans as they went into business together.

R.A. Gibbs was capped 16 times for Wales during a career between 1901 and 1911, in which he made 130 appearances for Cardiff, scored 90 tries, and was captain in 1910/11, before he retired. He played against the New Zealanders when Cardiff went close to beating them in the club's most successful season of 1905/06 and made the record books in 1908 when he scored four tries for Wales against France. It could have been more – on one occasion, when already over the French line, he tried to run round between the posts and was tackled without being able to ground the ball.

Three

Success on a World Stage

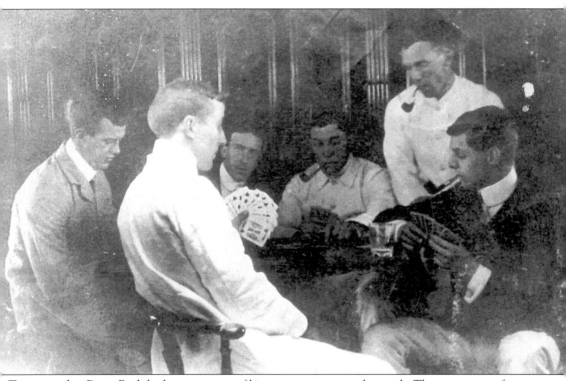

Trump cards – Percy Bush looks on as some of his new team-mates play cards. They were part of the 1904 British team (later to be known as the British Lions) on board the SS *Ormoz* heading for Australia and New Zealand. Another member of the team which was to win all fourteen games in Australia but who were less successful in New Zealand, losing the only Test in Wellington, was Rhys Gabe. In the following year, the All Blacks arrived in Wales, to be followed by the Springboks and Wallabies, heralding several seasons of epic matches at Cardiff Arms Park against both Cardiff and Wales.

Gwyn Nicholls captained Wales to one of their most famous victories – against the 1905 New Zealand team – to which a corner of the Cardiff trophy room is dedicated (see page 50).

Four Cardiff backs were involved in that memorable win: Gwyn Nicholls, H.B. Winfield, R.T. Gabe and Percy Bush, the club captain who was winning his first cap. The other backs were: Willie Llewellyn of Peny graig and E.T. Morgan of London Welsh, who scored the winning try. In fact, the Welsh Rugby Union had asked that both Llewellyn and Morgan should play for Cardiff alongside the four at Blackheath on the previous Saturday, 9 December, a request that was happily accepted: Cardiff won 24-4.

NUMBERS, NAMES AND POSITIONS OF PLAYERS.

NEW ZEALAND v. WALES.

NEW ZEALAND.	Kick off 2.30 p.m.	WALES.

BACK—

15 G. GILLETT (Canterbury).

THREE-QUARTER BACKS—

14 W. J. WALLACE (Wellington).
13 R. G. DEANS (Canterbury).
12 D. M'GREGOR (Wellington).

FIVE-EIGHTHS—

11 H. J. MYNOTT (Taranaki).
10 J. HUNTER (Taranaki).

HALF BACK—

9 J. ROBERTS (Wellington).

FORWARDS—

8 S. CASEY (Otago).
7 F. GLASGOW (Taranaki).
6 F. NEWTON (Canterbury).
5 J. O'SULLIVAN (Taranaki).
4 G. TYLER (Auckland).
3 A. M'DONALD (Otago).
2 C. SEELING (Auckland).
1 D. GALLAHER (*Wing*, Capt., Auckland).

BACK—

1 H. B. WINFIELD (Cardiff).

THREE-QUARTER BACKS—

2 E. G. NICHOLLS (Captain, Cardiff).
3 WILLIE LLEWELLYN (Penygraig).
4 R. T. GABE (Cardiff).
5 E. T. MORGAN (London Welsh).

HALF BACKS—

6 R. M. OWEN (Swansea).
7 PERCY BUSH (Cardiff).

EXTRA BACK—

8 CLIFF PRITCHARD (Pontypool).

FORWARDS—

9 W. JOSEPH (Swansea).
10 G. TRAVERS (Pill Harriers).
11 J. J. HODGES (Newport).
12 C. M. PRITCHARD (Newport).
13 A. F. HARDING (London Welsh).
14 J. F. WILLIAMS (London Welsh).
15 D. JONES (Aberdare),

Referee—MR DALLAS (Scotland).

Linesmen—MR. G. H. DIXON (President New Zealand Team), MR. ACK LLEWELLYN (Pontypridd).

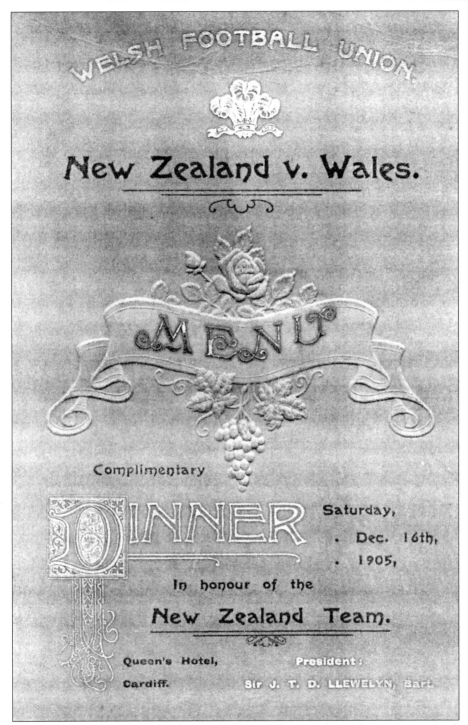

WELSH FOOTBALL UNION.

New Zealand v. Wales.

MENU

Complimentary

DINNER

Saturday,
Dec. 16th,
1905,

In honour of the

New Zealand Team.

Queen's Hotel,
Cardiff.

President:
Sir J. T. D. LLEWELYN, Bart.

The dinner in the Queen's Hotel in Westgate Street following the Wales *v.* New Zealand match was a sumptuous affair. The menu included native oysters, fillets of sole mornay, fried smelts, chicken saute or casserole, boiled turkey, pheasants, wild duck and seddon pudding with brandy sauce.

E. G. NICHOLLS.

Gwyn Nicholls, quite apart from captaining the club for four seasons and scoring 111 tries in his 242 appearances for Cardiff between 1892 and 1910, during which he was also capped 24 times by Wales, went on the British tour to Australia in 1899 and later served for many years on both Cardiff and WRU committees. The illustrations show him as depicted by Churchman's in their cigarette card series, as a WRU selector in 1926/27 and his signature among many famous players on the menu of the Wales v. Scotland match that season.

Canny Scot: "Eh mon! but you have me at a disadvantage here, I'm telling ye."

(Hamish Stuart gives it as his opinion that Scotland would stand a better chance if the game could be fought on other than Welsh soil.)

The cartoonist's name – C.W. Nicholls – may be just coincidence, but his view shows Gwyn Nicholls repelling Scottish invaders before the international in February 1906.

THE OFFICIAL
PROGRAMME.

New Zealand

v.

Cardiff

Cardiff Arms Park,
Boxing–day, Dec. 26th, 1905.

Printed and Published by Rees' Electric Press, Plymouth Street, Cardiff

The programme cover cannot tell the story but, when New Zealand played Cardiff on Boxing Day 1905, it was only ten days after the memorable win by Wales and the club went close to emulating the national side. The All Blacks, who lost just the one match during their thirty-five match tour, in which they scored 970 points against 59, won 10-8 and it was a rare, sad and costly mistake by the captain Percy Bush that tipped the balance. Cardiff had taken the lead with a try by Nicholls, converted by Winfield, only for the visitors to equalise by the interval. Then, an innocuous kick ahead over the line saw Bush unaccountably hesitate before minoring the ball. The New Zealanders pounced, scored, converted and, although Cardiff did manage a second try through Ralph Thomas in the corner, Winfield could not convert and the game was lost. It was in fact the only time Cardiff were beaten in thirty-two matches that season.

The teams in the programme of the
Cardiff *v.* New Zealand match, which the
visitors so fortuitously won.

Nos., Names and Positions of Players.

NEW ZEALAND.

BACK—
1   W. J. WALLACE (Wellington).
THREE-QUARTER BACKS—
2   THOMPSON
3   R. G. DEANS (Canterbury).
4   E. BOOTH.
FIVE-EIGHTHS—
5   J. W. STEAD.
6   J. HUNTER (Taranaki).
HALF-BACK—
7   J. ROBERTS (Wellington).
FORWARDS—
8   S. CASEY (Otago).
9   D. GALLAHER (Auckland).
    (Capt.)
10   F. GLASGOW (Taranaki).
11   F. NEWTON (Canterbury).
12   G. NICHOLSON.
13   C. SEELING (Auckland).
14   A. M'DONALD (Otago).
15   G. GILLETT (Canterbury).

CARDIFF.

BACK—H. B. WINFIELD.
THREE-QUARTER BACKS—
R. T. GABE,   E. G. NICHOLLS,
J. L. WILLIAMS,   R. C. THOMAS.
EXTRA BACK—R. GIBBS.
HALF BACKS—P. BUSH (Capt.), R. DAVID.
FORWARDS—
G. NORTHMORE,   W. NEILL.
J. POWELL,   J. BROWN,   F. SMITH,
L. GEORGE,   E. RUMBELOW.

CARDIFF FOOTBALL CLUB.

New Zealand *v.* Cardiff

GRAND STAND SIDE

AT CARDIFF ARMS PARK, CARDIFF,

BOXING DAY, December 26th, 1905, kick off 2.30 p.m.

ADMIT TO SEATS
INSIDE THE ROPES.   Ticket **3/-**   *Reserved (Not Numbered).*

NOTE.—All the Stands have been substantially erected and have been carefully
examined but all tickets of admission issued by the Cardiff Football Club for any
Football Match are issued upon the condition that the holder shall have no
remedy against the said Club its Committee or Members for injury sustained in
consequence of over-crowding of the Ground or Stands or in any way attributable
to the conduct or behaviour of any of the spectators,

N.B.—This Ticket
must not be given
up, but kept by
the owner as a
voucher for seat.

Chas. S. Arthur

ENTRANCE :—
GATE NEAR COUNTY CLUB.   *Secretary.*

A ticket for a reserved but
unnumbered seat within the
'ropes' for the
Cardiff *v.* New Zealand
match cost three shillings.

The Hubert Johnson Trophy Room in the Cardiff clubhouse has a corner devoted to the memorabilia of players concerning the Wales *v.* New Zealand match – and especially the controversy surrounding a try disallowed against Deans, the New Zealand wing, which is depicted in the painting by Alan Brinkworth (below).

Cigarette cards proliferated and three Cardiff men who featured on them – 'John Alf' Brown (above), Fred Smith (above right) and John Powell (right) – played for Cardiff against the New Zealanders and, the following year, in the side that beat the South Africans. Brown, also known as 'Big John', won 7 caps for Wales, played 221 times for Cardiff and was Rhys Gabe's vice-captain in 1907/08. His son, Duncan, was to make 93 appearances for the club between 1931 and 1939 and was later still to serve on the rugby committee. Police sergeant Fred Smith was uncapped but played 175 matches for Cardiff while Powell won a single cap and made 164 club appearances.

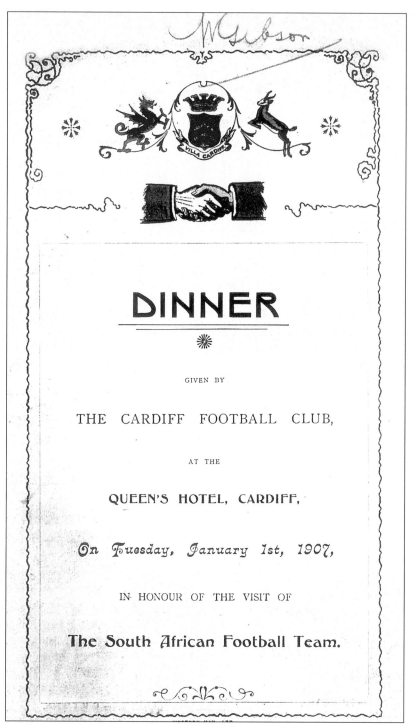

DINNER

GIVEN BY

THE CARDIFF FOOTBALL CLUB,

AT THE

QUEEN'S HOTEL, CARDIFF,

On Tuesday, January 1st, 1907,

IN HONOUR OF THE VISIT OF

The South African Football Team.

The first South Africans came to Cardiff for the penultimate match of their tour on New Year's Day 1907, having lost only to Scotland. Cardiff must have enjoyed this after-match dinner as they won 17-0 in muddy conditions. The following week, the Springboks completed their twenty-nine match tour with a 13-tries demolition of France in Paris.

Cardiff 17 points. Cardiff v. South Africans. Jany. 1. 1907. South Africans NIL

The Cardiff team that beat the South Africans with tries by Gwyn Nicholls, R.A. Gibbs, J.L. Williams and R.T. Gabe, with Bert Winfield kicking a conversion and a penalty. 'No Cardiff team ever played better or achieved so great renown', wrote the club's secretary and historian, Charles Arthur.

A rare action picture from the match, after which the South Africans said that Cardiff were a great team of gentlemen and athletes.

THE AUSTRALIANS'

WAR SONG

••

Gau Gau — Cardiff — Gau Gau — Cardiff —
Whir-r-r
Win nang-a-lang (Thur)
Mu-e-an-yil-ling.
Bu rang-a-lang (Yang).
Yai yai. Gun-yil-lang-yang-yah

The next overseas visitors to appear against Cardiff were the Australians and, despite the 'War Chant' printed on the after-match dinner menu, they were beaten 24-8.

J. L. WILLIAMS.   L. M. DYKE.   H. B. WINFIELD (injured).   W. SPILLER.   R. A. GIBBS.
Deputised by R. WILLIAMS.

J. BROWN   W. L. MORGAN.   P. F. BUSH (Capt.)   F. SMITH (Vice-Capt.)

J. POWELL.   J. CASEY.   D. WESTACOTT.   J. PUGSLEY.   F. GACCON.   G. YEWLETT.

The Cardiff team which, on 28 December 1908, gave the Australians the heaviest defeat of their tour. All of Cardiff's 24 points were scored by the backs: J.L. Williams scored two tries, with one apiece from Louis Dyke, W.L. Morgan and Rhys Gabe, while Percy Bush converted one besides kicking a penalty and a drop goal.

The teams from the programme of that successful December day.

Teams

	Australia		Cardiff
	Full Back—		*Full Back—*
14	P. CARMICHAEL	2	R. WILLIAMS
	Threequarter Backs—		*Threequarter Backs—*
12	C. RUSSELL, Right Wing	6	J. L. WILLIAMS, Left Wing
16	J. HICKEY, Inside	5	L. M. DYKE, Left Centre
15	E. F. MANDIBLE, Outside	4	W. SPILLER, Right Centre
11	F. BEDE SMITH, Left Wing	3	R. A. GIBBS, Right Wing
	Five-Eighth—		*Half Backs—*
10	C. H. McKIVAT	1	P. F. BUSH, Capt., Outside
	Half Back—		
9	F. WOODS	7	W. L. MORGAN, Inside
	Forwards—		*Forwards—*
1	DR. MORAN, Capt.	8	F. SMITH
2	S. A. MIDDLETON	9	J. BROWN
3	M. McARTHUR	10	J. POWELL
4	A. B. BURGE	11	J. CASEY
5	J. T. BARNETT	12	D. WESTACOTT
6	P. McCUE	14	F. GACCON
7	N. E. ROW	15	G. YEWLETT
8	C. C. HAMMOND	16	J. PUGSLEY

DR. H M MORAN
CAPT.
AUSTRALIA

MR. P. F. BUSH
CAPT.
CARDIFF

DINNER

to Commemorate
the Visit of the
Australian Rugby
Football Team,
at Queen's Hotel,
Cardiff, Monday,
December 28, 1908

A Souvenir

Rees' Electric Press,
Plymouth St., Cardiff.

Once more, the Cardiff team would have enjoyed their sumptuous feast following a fine win against a touring team.

History was not to repeat itself when the second Springboks came to the Arms Park in December 1912 and Cardiff went down 7-6. Cardiff scored the only try of the match through the captain, Billy Spiller, and even though Johnny Rogers also kicked a penalty goal, the six points were not enough to beat the South Africans, who won through a drop goal (four points) and a penalty.

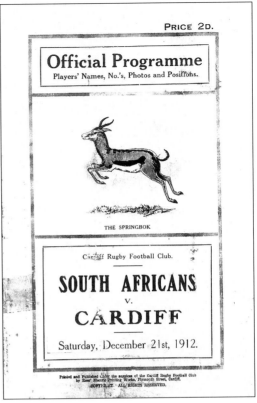

Billy Spiller, a Glamorgan police sergeant who captained the club against the South Africans, also achieved fame in other ways. After playing 184 times for Cardiff and being in a Triple Crown-winning Welsh side whilst earning his 10 caps, he was later to score the first century for Glamorgan on their entry into first-class cricket.

WILL HISTORY REPEAT ITSELF?

Into the field the Springboks bound,
　　In fettle for the fray,
Galloping gaily round and round,
　　Scenting from far their prey.

Close at their heels come Cardiff's pack,
Still of the self-same strain
That beat the last 'boks " blue and black."
They never smiled again.

" History repeats itself " they say,
　　" To be or not to be ? "
Up with the penny ; heads or tails ?
　　'Tis wise to " wait and see."

The match programme for that second Springbok game asked the question – and the answer was 'no'. It was just as well that the writer suggested that it was wise to 'wait and see'!

AFTER THE MATCH.

Great BOXING Tournament

AT

THEATRE ROYAL, St. Mary Street

Great TWELVE ROUND Contest

JIMMY WILDE, The Little Welsh Wonder,

v.

BILLY YATES, BARGOED, Winner of over 30 Contests.
And other important events.

JIM DRISCOLL, The Feather-weight Champion of the World, will positively appear and Box

TEN ROUNDS with Joe Johns, Bat McCarthy and Badger Brien.

Doors open at 6, Commence at **6.45**. **POPULAR PRICES, 1/- to 5/-**

The programme also suggested some post-match entertainment at the Theatre Royal, where Jimmy Wilde was topping a boxing bill that also boasted Jim Driscoll. Note that the featherweight champion of the World will 'positively appear and box ten rounds' against three opponents.

Four

A Decade of Glory

The *annus mirabilis* of Welsh rugby, with the epic 3-0 defeat of New Zealand, was also the Cardiff club's greatest season. Captained by Percy Bush, and including great players such as Gwyn Nicholls, Rhys Gabe, Winfield, Gibbs and John Williams, the team were beaten only once (by the All Blacks) in 32 games. It was, by any standards, a golden period. Between September 1905 and April 1909 the club were beaten only 11 times in 126 games.

Percy Frank Bush was one of the greatest players in the history of Cardiff, Welsh and British rugby. Born in 1879, he went with clubmate Rhys Gabe on the British tour of Australia and New Zealand in 1904. Like Cliff Morgan with the Lions in South Africa half a century later, Percy Bush was the team's supreme playmaker at fly-half and attracted admiring crowds wherever he went. Back home in Wales, he helped the national side beat New Zealand in 1905 and then led Cardiff to victories over South Africa in 1907 and Australia in 1908. One of the club's most successful captains, he scored 66 tries and 35 dropped goals in 171 games for Cardiff, as well as playing cricket for Glamorgan.

This very early example of action photography shows Percy Bush scoring one of his 66 tries for the club.

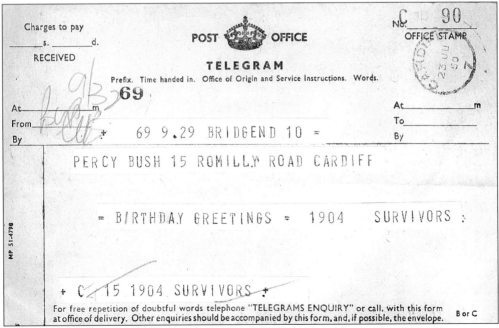

A birthday telegram to Percy Bush, typical of the camaraderie of rugby. The 1904 Survivors are presumably from the British Tour of New Zealand and Australia.

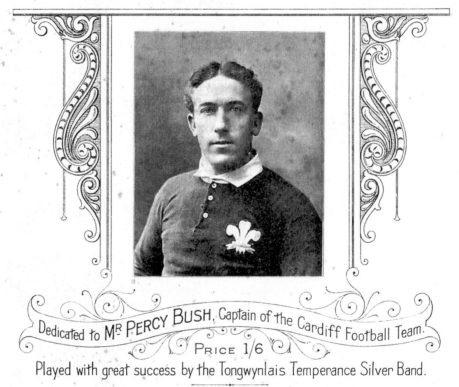

"CAPTAIN BUSH MARCH"

for PIANO

BY

ADOLPHUS W. DAVIES.

Dedicated to Mr PERCY BUSH, Captain of the Cardiff Football Team.

PRICE 1/6

Played with great success by the Tongwynlais Temperance Silver Band.

Published by the Composer.
CASTLE ROAD, TONGWYNLAIS. NEAR CARDIFF.

Full Brass Band Parts may be had of above March.
Also by same Composer, Baritone or Contralto Solo, "TO THEE, MY GOD AND SAVIOUR." Price 1/- post free.

An indication of the high regard in which Percy Bush was held is the composition of the 'Captain Bush March' by Adolphus W. Davies of Tongwynlais. This would have appealed to the theatrical side of Percy's nature: he was a notorious comic off the field of play – and some would say on it! A rare copy of the sheet music is deposited in the Cardiff Rugby Club Museum.

PERCY BUSH, du S. N. U. C.

Percy Bush won 8 caps for Wales. Having spent three seasons as club captain, he moved to France in 1910, where he became a consular official and, eventually, a British vice-consul in Nantes. During that time he played for the Stade Nantais Universite Club and scored 54 points, including 10 tries in a game against Le Havre. The French always held Percy in the highest regard and awarded him the Medaille d'Argent de la Reconaissance in 1952. As these contemporary illustrations show, French newspapers and magazines regularly published his caricature and portrait throughout his time in France. Percy Bush returned to Wales before the Second World War and died in Cardiff in 1955.

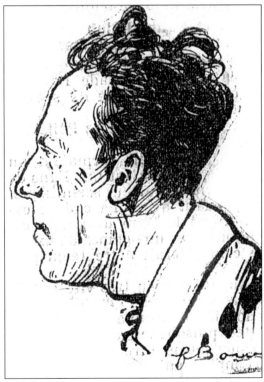

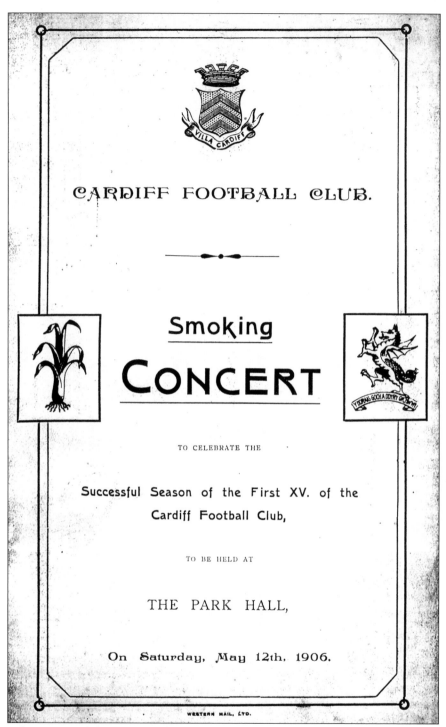

CARDIFF FOOTBALL CLUB.

Smoking

CONCERT

TO CELEBRATE THE

Successful Season of the First XV. of the
Cardiff Football Club,

TO BE HELD AT

THE PARK HALL,

On Saturday, May 12th, 1906.

WESTERN MAIL, LTD.

Never reluctant to celebrate great achievements in style, the 'Cardiff Football Club', under the chairmanship of W.D. Phillips, held a Smoking Concert at the Park Hotel at the end of the great season of 1905/06. With the agreement of the Welsh Rugby Union, gold watches were presented to each of the twenty-one players.

✳ ✳ ✳

. Programme .

First Part.	Second Part.
1—Song Mr. Harry Williams.	1—Part Song ... ... "In absence" Cardiff Male Voice Party. Conductor, Mr. Roderick Williams.
2—Comic Song ... ... "Simple little Sister, Mary Green" Mr. E. Williams.	2—Musical Monologue ... ... "My Old Clay Pipe" Mr. H. Quiningborough.
3—Song ... ... "Blodwen, my Darling" Mr. J. Games.	3—Concertina Solo Mr. R. T. Chinn.
4—Welsh Air ... ... "Llwyn Onn" Cardiff Male Voice Party. Conductor, Mr. Roderick Williams.	4—Whistling Song Mr. Tony Lucas.
5—Comic Song ... ... "There isn't much more to say" Mr. Tony Lucas.	5—Prestidigitation Mr. Charles Oswald.
6—Clarionique ... The Clarion Harmony Quartette.	6—Song ... ... "Queen of the Earth" Mr. J. F. Proud.
7—Humorous Song ... ... "Logic" Mr. H. Quiningborough.	7—Comic Song ... ... "Ha! Ha!! Ha!!!" Mr. Donald Ross.
8—Duet ... ... "Excelsior" Messrs. W. E. Carston and J. F. Proud.	8—Song ... ... "Mary" Mr. W. E. Carston.
9—Comic Song ... ... "The Softest of the Family" Mr. Donald Ross.	9—Comic Song ... ... "Good Bye, Eliza Jane" Mr. E. Williams.
10—Song ... ... "Good Company" Mr. W. E. Carston.	10—Welsh Air ... ... "Ar hyd y Nos" Cardiff Male Voice Party. Conductor, Mr. Roderick Williams.

Toast - CARDIFF FOOTBALL TEAM.

Proposer - The President.
Responder - Mr. P. F. Bush, Captain.

Accompanist - - Mr. FRANK HOOPER.

The programme for the Smoking Concert shows the true essence of an Edwardian evening, with several solo artists, a harmony quartet and, of course, a male voice choir. Presumably, there was a subtle difference between the 'Humorous Song' of Mr H. Quiningborough and the 'Comic Song' of Mr Donald Ross and others!

The full extent of the First XV's achievement is reflected in the end of season's fixture list. Old rivals such as Newport and Swansea were each beaten four times and the Barbarians twice. In the Easter Saturday match, J.L. Williams scored five tries in what the Baa-Baa's own records – believing they had fielded a strong team – described as a 'bit of a drubbing'.

Record of the 1st XV., Season 1905-6.

DATE.	OPPONENTS.	RESULT.	WHERE PLAYED.	SCORE FOR. G.	T.	PTS.	AGAINST. G.	T.	PTS.
Sept. 23	Cardiff & District	Won	Home	*§3	2	19	0	0	0
30	Penarth	"	Home	§3	1	11	†1	1	6
Oct. 7	Bristol	"	Away	*1	0	4	0	1	3
14	Newport	"	Away	"	*3	1	14	0	1	3
21	Swansea	"	Home	*†*3	1	14	0	1	3
28	Gloucester	Drawn	Home	"	0	1	3	0	1	3
Nov. 4	Devonport	Won	Home	*2	1	12	0	0	0
11	Llanelly	"	Away	0	1	3	0	0	0
18	Newport	"	Home	1	3	14	0	2	6
25	Swansea	"	Away	*†2	0	7	0	0	0
Dec. 9	Blackheath	"	Away	§3	2	24	*1	0	4
23	London Welsh	"	Home	1	3	14	†.	0	5
26	New Zealand	Lost	Home	1	1	8	2	0	10
27	Barbarians	Won	Home	3	0	15	0	0	0
30	Old Merchant Taylors	"	Home	2	6	28	0	0	0
Jan. 6	Moseley	"	Away	2	2	16	*†2	0	7
13	Aberavon	"	Home	1	6	23	0	0	0
20	Bristol	"	Home	3	5	30	1	3	11
27	Blackheath	"	Home	2	2	16	0	0	0
Feb. 10	Moseley	"	Home	4	4	32	0	0	0
17	Newport	"	Away	*1	2	10	0	1	3
24	Swansea	"	Home	3	0	15	0	1	3
27	Paris	"	Away	*2	6	27	1	0	5
Mar. 3	Leicester	Drawn	Away	0	1	3	0	1	3
10	Neath	Won	Home	1	1	8	0	1	3
17	Newport	"	Home	*†1	1	9	0	0	0
24	Swansea	"	Away	0	1	3	0	0	0
31	Gloucester	"	Home	*2	2	15	0	0	0
April 7	Devonport	"	Away	1	2	11	0	1	3
14	Barbarians	"	Home	†5	5	38	0	0	0
16	Leicester	"	Home	2	1	13	0	0	0
21	Llanelly	"	Home	*4	7	40	0	0	0
				65	71	513	10	14	86

* Dropped Goal. † Penalty Goal. § Mark Goal.

Played 32. Won 29. Drawn 2. Lost 1.

TRY GETTERS:—J. L. Williams, 35; C. F. Biggs, 17; P. F. Bush, 11; R. A. Gibbs, 10; E. G. Nicholls, 9; R. T. Gabe, 8; R. C. Thomas, 6; G. Northmore, 3; J. Powell, 3; G. McCraith, 3; J. Brown, 2; J. Pugsley, 2; D. Westacott, 1; R. J. David, 1; W. A. Jones, 1; D. L. Evans, 1; R. Davies, 1; W. H. Pullen, 1; W. Neill, 1; E. Rumbelow, 1; and L. S. Thomas, 1.

DROPPED GOALS:—P. F. Bush, 6; R. C. Thomas, 3; C. F. Biggs, 1; E. G. Nicholls, 1.

PENALTY GOALS:—H. B. Winfield, 6; P. F. Bush, 1.

In some respects, Rhys Gabe's playing career was even more distinguished than that of Percy Bush. A fellow British tourist to the Antipodes in 1904, Gabe was also club captain in 1907/08 and, in total, scored 51 tries in 115 games for Cardiff. His 24 caps for Wales included the win over New Zealand in 1905 and the following season he played against the touring Springboks on four occasions – for Glamorgan, Wales, Llanelli and Cardiff.

The report of Cardiff's victory at Moseley, on 9 November 1907, relates the extraordinary tale of Rhys Gabe's prophetic dream on the eve of the match about the non-arrival of Edgar Thomas on the following morning.

CARDIFF'S GOOD FORM.

SPARKLING EXHIBITION AT MOSELEY.

[By FENDRAGON.]

	G.	T.	Pts.
Cardiff	2	3	19
Moseley	0	0	0

It is to be hoped that Cardiff's form at Moseley on Saturday was prophetic of even better things to come. Playing without H. B. Winfield, J. L. Williams, R. A. Gibbs, P. F. Bush, and J. Pugsley, they scored a decisive victory over the strongest side the Midland club could put in the field.

That was a happy idea which occurred to Rhys Gabe during a dream on Friday night. In his hours of slumber the Cardiff skipper dreamt that Edgar Thomas had not come up by the morning train as intended, and that he himself was playing outside half. The vision came absolutely true, for Edgar Thomas did not arrive, and Gabe did actually play at outside half. Well it was that he did so, for he gave a thoroughly good display, such a display as a man of Gabe's build would hardly be expected to give in that position.

Cardiff's first score came after a great burst by Gabe, who sent Ralph Thomas, W. A. Jones, and M'Oraith careering for the line with only two men to beat. When Jones received from Thomas he did not find it necessary to pass to M'Oraith, for the left centre went over the line in the grasp of the full-back.

Jones and M'Oraith were bringing off a lot of clever work on the left, and after the wing man had made several fine runs, he showed the acme of judgment when he drew three or four opponents upon him, and, suddenly stopping dead, gave a sharp pass to Gabe, who was left with no one to beat.

The next try was a beauty. David fed Gabe so cleverly that the skipper was running at top speed when he received the ball. In a twinkling he was clear of the halves and three-quarters, and easily beating the full-back, he scored behind the posts for Frank Wood to convert.

Well fed by their talented inside half-back, David, with Gabe doing well as his partner, the Cardiff three-quarters were seen to excellent advantage, and indulged in many brilliant bouts of passing, but Moseley, as usual, offered a stubborn resistance—Moseley are nothing if they are not a strong defensive side. Wilson, their full-back, defended so ably, and his efforts were so well seconded by those of Cooper and Birtles, that 29 minutes elapsed before Cardiff got going. When, however, the Moseley line was once crossed, the Welshmen took a great deal of keeping out. Gabe, prior to getting slightly hurt, was easily the cleverest man in the game, although McCraith was speedy and clever, and some of his runs were only unproductive by reason of dire ill-luck following the footsteps of this particular player. So the game went on, Moseley generally having to be content to act on the defensive.

With a weakened team, Cardiff's form was decidedly pleasing, while Gabe at outside half was quite a startling success. Certainly, he is the only man I have seen in that position who can take David's cannon-ball passes equally as well as Percy Bush. Several times he took the ball when full on

54

A cartoon that suitably marks Neath's 5-3 victory at the Gnoll on 8 February 1908. It was only Cardiff's second defeat of the season so far, but Rhys Gabe was quick to congratulate the Welsh All Blacks on the splendid reception given to the Cardiff team and for winning a 'clean and clever game'.

Cardiff had welcomed the Cardiff & District XV to the Arms Park since 1882 and, by the time of this game in 1906, the fixture was well-established as the pipe-opener to the new season. The buildings of Westgate Street provide an impressive backdrop to the play on the pitch.

Cardiff Football Club

FIXTURES 1908-9

VILLA CARDIFF

FIXTURES 1908-9

FIRST TEAM			RESERVES		
1908	NAME OF CLUB	GROUND	**1908**	NAME OF CLUB	GROUND
Sept. 12	Practice	Home	Sept. 12	Weston-super-Mare	Home
,, 19	Cardiff and District	Home	,, 19	Taunton Albion	Home
,, 26	Neath	Home W 10-3	,, 26	Neath 2nds ...	Away
Oct. 3	Bristol	Away W.	Oct. 3	Bristol Nomads	Home
,, 10	Newport	Home W 15-8	,, 10	Newport 2nds	Away
,, 17	Swansea	Away	,, 17	Swansea 2nds	Home
,, 24	Gloucester	Home	,, 24	Gloucester 2nds	Away
,, 26	Pontypool	Away	,, 31	Risca	Home
,, 31	Leicester	Away	Nov. 7	Moseley 2nds	Away
Nov. 7	Moseley	Home	,, 14	Newport 2nds	Home
,, 14	Newport	Away	,, 21	Swansea 2nds	Away
,, 21	Swansea	Home	,, 28	Neath 2nds	Home
,, 28	Neath	Away	Dec. 5	Chepstow	Home
Dec. 5	Blackheath	Away	,, 12	**N. S. WALES v. WALES**	Wales
,, 12	**N. S. WALES v. WALES** ,	Wales	,, 19	Abergavenny	Away
,, 19	Llanelly	Home	**1909**		
,, *26	Barbarians	Home	Jan. 2	Penarth 2nds	Away
,, †28	New South Wales	Home	,, 9	Moseley 2nds	Home
1909			,, 16	**ENGLAND v. WALES**	Cardiff
Jan. 1	Glamorgan League	Home	,, 23	Risca	Away
,, 2	Penarth	Home	,, 30	Monmouth	Home
,, 9	Moseley	Away	Feb. 6	Cup Winners	Home
,, 16	**ENGLAND v. WALES**	Cardiff	,, 13	Newport 2nds	Away
,, 23	Blackheath	Home	,, 20	League Winners	Home
,, 30	Llanelly	Away	,, 27	Bristol Nomads	Away
Feb. 6	**SCOTLAND v. WALES** ...	Scot'd	Mar. 6	Newport 2nds	Home
,, 13	Newport	Home	,, 13	**IRELAND v. WALES**	Swansea
,, 20	Bordeaux	Away	,, 20	Chepstow	Away
,, 27	Bristol	Home	,, 27	Abergavenny	Home
Mar. 6	Newport	Away	Apr. 3	Gloucester 2nds	Home
,, 13	**IRELAND v. WALES**	Swansea	,, 10	Monmouth	Away
,, 17	Devonport Albion	Home	,, *12	Taunton Albion	Away
,, 20	Pontypool	Home	,, 13	Weston-super-Mare ...	Away
,, 27	London Welsh	Home	,, 17	Penylan	Home
Apr. 3	Gloucester	Away			
,, 10	Leicester	Home			
,, *12	Barbarians	Home			
,, 17	Devonport Albion	Away			

* Bank Holidays

† This Match is not one of the Club Matches referred to in Bye-Law 7.

| PERCY F. BUSH, Captain | C. S. ARTHUR, Secretary, 53 Queen Street | G. NORTHMORE, Captain |

A fixture list to bring tears of joy to both the supporters and the club treasurer. Regular Saturday afternoon rugby, twenty home matches, and the Barbarians at the Arms Park over Christmas and Easter. The matches listed as New South Wales against Wales and Cardiff in December 1908 were, in fact, games against Australia. Wales won 9-6, but Cardiff went one better with a 24-8 victory – the Wallabies' biggest defeat of their thirty-one match tour.

Cardiff first played in Ireland in 1907, taking on the Constitution Club in Cork on 29 April. The team photograph shows Percy Bush alongside the home skipper, D. Desmond.

There was great excitement surrounding the visit, the local *Cork Examiner* describing Cardiff as 'the finest club team in the world'.

A crowd of 10,000 packed in to the Mardyke Football Grounds to see the visitors win 19-3, with a performance that the *Examiner* described as 'a piece of perfection, a faultless piece of mechanism, and they seem incapable of erring, except by accident'.

THE RACE FOR THE WELSH CLUB CHAMPIONSHIP.
A Long Stride by Black Bess Holds Up the Favourite.

Throughout the 1900s, the intense rivalry amongst the senior Welsh clubs was represented in newspaper cartoons. The teams were sometimes shown as racehorses and at other times as dames.

"There's many a slip
'Twixt the cup and the lip."

DAME NEWPORT (the Guest) :—Greedy thing! After offering it to me to snatch it away just when I was goi g to drink! I thought at least to have a DRAW out of it. Last Saturday, Cardiff snatched a victory in the last minute. Newport had hard lines in not drawing the game.

Here, the Cardiff Club is portrayed as 'Burglar Bill', about to snatch the Welsh Club Championship after Newport could only draw a match with Swansea.

UP HIS SLEEVE.

P.C. : Hi! What's that 'ere up yer sleeve ?
BILL CARDIFF : This 'ere's the Welsh Club Championship, ole feller.
(Newport's draw with Swansea last Saturday makes Cardiff's chances of the Welsh Club Championship still more certain.)

THE WELSH CLUB CHAMPIONSHIP PLATE.

Swansea, with Trew in his best form, shows the way in rare style.

But finally, despite the best efforts of Cardiff and Newport, Swansea emerge as clear favourites. For them, there was no finer 'jockey' than Billy Trew, a great competitor against Cardiff, whose 29 caps for Wales included four Grand Slams and three Triple Crowns – clearly marking him a winner.

61

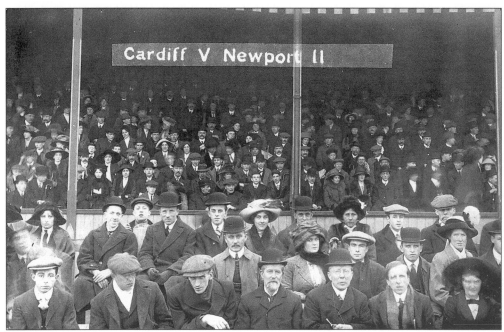

These photographs from 1908 and 1910 show the crowds packed into the stands to watch games against Newport and Leicester. Ladies' membership tickets were available and the ladies are certainly well represented in the crowds for these home games.

CARDIFF V LLANELLY I

A fascinating picture of family support for the club emerges: the Mitchells and Bickleys have watched Cardiff play for ninety years, right up to the modern era. William Mitchell, Margaret Bickley and Margaret Mitchell have been identified in the second row of spectators at the match against Llanelly – the two Margarets are joined by Mary Goodwin-Bickley (they are the three ladies in splendid hats in the back row) for the game against the Barbarians.

Cardiff V Barbarians. 13

Cardiff first played Moseley in December 1880 and had established regular home and away fixtures by 1885/86. This game, in November 1908, which Cardiff won 8-0, provides an early example of a programme for a club match. Printed on fine card and folded to create six pages, it includes 'The Week's Football Gossip' by 'Blind-side' and is not short on opinion – the club's loss of its unbeaten record to Leicester the previous week was attributed to 'Mr Referee [when] Cardiff were in the Cart-wright throughout the game'!

The OFFICIAL Programme

Published under the Auspices of the Cardiff Rugby F.C.

Cardiff Arms Park.
_____

Moseley v. Cardiff

Saturday, November 7th.

REES' ELECTRIC PRESS, PLYMOUTH STREET, CARDIFF.

Price One Penny

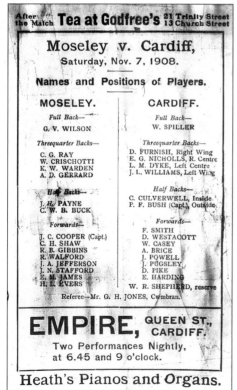

After the Match **Tea at Godfree's** 21 Trinity Street 13 Church Street

Moseley v. Cardiff,
Saturday, Nov. 7, 1908.

Names and Positions of Players.

MOSELEY.	CARDIFF.
Full Back—	*Full Back—*
G. V. WILSON	W. SPILLER
Threequarter Backs—	*Threequarter Backs—*
C. G. RAY	D. FURNISH, Right Wing
W. CRISCHOTTI	E. G. NICHOLLS, R. Centre
K. W. WARDEN	L. M. DYKE, Left Centre
A. D. GERRARD	J. L. WILLIAMS, Left Wing
Half Backs—	*Half Backs—*
J. H. PAYNE	C. CULVERWELL, Inside
C. W. B. BUCK	P. F. BUSH (Capt.), Outside
Forwards—	*Forwards—*
	F. SMITH
J. C. COOPER (Capt.)	D. WESTACOTT
C. H. SHAW	W. CASEY
R. B. GIBBINS	A. BRICE
R. WALFORD	J. POWELL
J. A. JEFFERSON	J. PUGSLEY
J. N. STAFFORD	D. PIKE
E. M. JAMES	E. HARDING
H. L. EVERS	W. R. SHEPHERD, reserve

Referee—Mr. G. H. JONES, Cwmbran.

EMPIRE, QUEEN ST., CARDIFF.
Two Performances Nightly,
at 6.45 and 9 o'clock.

Heath's Pianos and Organs.

8 POINTS ALL.

EICESTER v CARDIFF

AT CARDIFF ARMS PARK

SATURDAY, APRIL 10TH 1909.

The games against Leicester were a popular Anglo-Welsh encounter and Cardiff did not lose at home to the Tigers until 1920. The excellent action photograph, showing the architecture of Westgate Street before the blocks of flats were built, suggests that lifting in the lineout remained a tactic for the future.

Also in the 1908/09 season, the club arranged a match in Bordeaux. The trip was to cost nearly £300 and was to be criticised by some members as extravagant – but the team won 21-5 and increased Cardiff's reputation further.

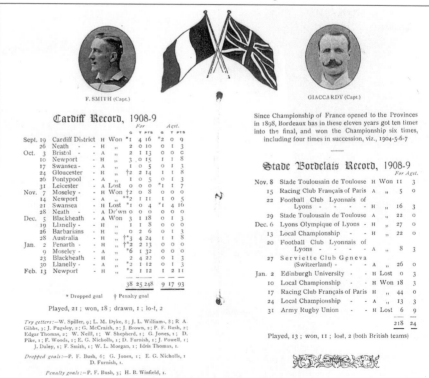

F. SMITH (Capt.)

GIACCARDY (Capt.)

Cardiff Record, 1908-9

				For			Agst.		
				G	T	PTS	G	T	PTS
Sept. 19	Cardiff District	H	Won	*1	4	16	*2	0	9
26	Neath - -	H	,,	2	0	10	0	1	3
Oct. 3	Bristol - -	A	,,	2	1	13	0	0	0
10	Newport -	H	,,	3	0	15	1	1	8
17	Swansea -	A	,,	1	0	5	0	1	3
24	Gloucester -	H	,,	†2	2	14	1	1	8
26	Pontypool -	A	,,	1	0	5	0	1	3
31	Leicester -	A	Lost	0	0	0	*1	1	7
Nov. 7	Moseley -	H	Won	†2	0	8	0	0	0
14	Newport -	A	,,	**2	1	11	1	0	5
21	Swansea -	A	Lost	*1	0	4	*1	4	16
28	Neath -	A	Dr'wn	0	0	0	0	0	0
Dec. 5	Blackheath -	A	Won	3	1	18	0	1	3
19	Llanelly -	H	,,	1	1	8	0	0	0
26	Barbarians -	H	,,	0	2	6	0	1	3
28	Australia -	H	,,	†*3	4	24	1	1	8
Jan. 2	Penarth -	H	,,	†*2	2	13	0	0	0
9	Moseley -	A	,,	*6	1	32	0	0	0
23	Blackheath -	H	,,	2	4	22	0	1	3
30	Llanelly -	A	,,	*2	1	12	0	1	3
Feb. 13	Newport -	H	,,	*2	1	12	1	2	11
				38	25	248	9	17	93

* Dropped goal   † Penalty goal

Played, 21 ; won, 18 ; drawn, 1 ; lost, 2

Try getters:—W. Spiller, 9; L. M. Dyke, 8; J. L. Williams, 8; R A. Gibbs, 3; J. Pugsley, 2; G. McCraith, 2; J. Brown, 2; P. F. Bush, 2; Edgar Thomas, 2; W. Neill, 1; W. Shepherd, 1; G. Jones, 1; D. Pike, 1; F. Woods, 1; E. G. Nicholls, 1; D. Furnish, 1; J. Powell, 1; J. Daley, 1; F. Smith, 1; W. L. Morgan, 1; Idris Thomas, 1.

Dropped goals:—P. F. Bush, 6; G. Jones, 1; E. G. Nicholls, 1 D. Furnish, 1.

Penalty goals:—P. F. Bush, 3; H. B. Winfield, 1.

Since Championship of France opened to the Provinces in 1898, Bordeaux has in these eleven years got ten times into the final, and won the Championship six times, including four times in succession, viz., 1904-5-6-7

Stade Bordelais Record, 1908-9

				For	Agst.
Nov. 8	Stade Toulousain de Toulouse	H	Won	11	3
15	Racing Club Français of Paris	A	,,	5	0
22	Football Club Lyonnais of Lyons - - -	H	,,	16	3
29	Stade Toulousain de Toulouse	A	,,	22	0
Dec. 6	Lyons Olympique of Lyons -	H	,,	27	0
13	Local Championship - -	H	,,	22	0
20	Football Club Lyonnais of Lyons - - -	A	,,	8	3
27	Serviette Club Geneva (Switzerland) - -	A	,,	26	0
Jan. 2	Edinburgh University - -	H	Lost	0	3
10	Local Championship - -	H	Won	18	3
17	Racing Club Français of Paris	H	,,	44	0
24	Local Championship - -	A	,,	13	3
31	Army Rugby Union - -	H	Lost	6	9
				218	24

Played, 13 ; won, 11 ; lost, 2 (both British teams)

Thursday, February 18th

Leave Cardiff (G.W.R)	-	-	-	10.0 a.m.
Dinner in Dining Car	-	-	-	12.0 noon
Arrive Paddington	-	-	-	1.0 p.m.

G.W.R. Buses meet Train.

Leave Charing Cross	-	-	-	2.20 ,,
Arrive Folkestone	-	-	-	4. 0 ,,
Boat leaves Folkestone	-	-	-	4.10 ,,

Cup of Tea for those who require it.

French Time

Arrive Boulogne	-	-	-	5.40 p.m.
Leave Boulogne	-	-	-	6.17 ,,
Dinner in Dining Car	-	-	-	7. 0 ,,
Arrive Paris (Gare du Nord)	-	-	-	9.15 ,,

Buses meet Train for Hotel St. Petersbourg.

Supper	-	-	-	11.30 ,,

Friday, February 19th

Breakfast	-	-	-	6.45 a.m.
Leave Paris (Quai d'Orsay)	-	-	-	7.50 ,,
Lunch in Dining Car	-	-	-	11.50 ,,
Arrive Bordeaux (St. Jean)	-	-	-	4.48 p.m.

Grand Hotel Francais Bus meets Train.

Dinner	-	-	-	5.30 ,,
Supper	-	-	-	11. 0 ,,

Saturday, February 20th

Breakfast	-	-	-	9.15 a.m.
Lunch	-	-	-	1.30 p.m.
Match, Kick-off	-	-	-	4. 0 ,,
Dinner at the Restaurant Grisch (at the invitation of the Bordeaux Club)	-		-	7.30 ,,
Supper	-	-	-	11.30 ,,

The detailed itinerary shows the true nature of the expedition – five days away, travel by rail, road and sea, and two nights in Bordeaux.

Itinerary (*continued*)

Sunday, February 21st

Breakfast	-	-	-	9.15 a.m.
Leave Bordeaux (St. Jean)	-	-	-	11. 4 ,,
Lunch in Dining Car	-	-	-	12.50 p.m.
Arrive Paris (Quai d'Orsay)	-	-	-	6.15 ,,
Dinner	-	-	-	7. 0 ,,
Supper	-	-	-	11.30 ,,

Monday, February 22nd

Breakfast	-	-	-	7.15 a m.
Leave Paris (Gare du Nord)	-	-	-	8.25 ,,
Arrive Boulogne	-	-	-	11.45 ,,
Boat leaves Boulogne	-	-	-	12. 5 p.m.

Lunch on Boat.

Arrive Folkestone	-	-	-	1.30 ,,
Leave Folkestone	-	-	-	1.45 ,,
Arrive Charing Cross	-	-	-	3 34 ,,

G.W.R. Bus meets Train for Paddington.

Leave Paddington	-	-	-	6.10 ,,
Dinner in Dining Car	-	-	-	6.15 ,,
Arrive Cardiff	-	-	-	9.15 ,,

Charles Culverwell of St Fagans played scrum-half for Cardiff in 19 matches from 1908 to 1911. These extracts from his scrapbook show not only the action from a Cardiff *v.* Newport encounter of 1910, but also the huge crowds that attended, even in those days. Pendragon's report of a match that attracted 30,000 fans and ended in a scoreless draw covers not only the ebb and flow of the play but the weather conditions in great detail and the history of Cardiff *v.* Newport games.

30,000 PEOPLE

1909-10
5 March 1910

WATCH CARDIFF V. NEWPORT

GREAT TUSSLE

ENDS IN DRAWN BATTLE

GAME PLAYED IN GOOD SPIRIT

Final score:	G.	T.	Pts.
Cardiff	0	0	0
Newport	0	0	0

[By "PENDRAGON."]

Sunshine at last! Well, we wanted it, for this has been an atrocious winter. Since the season began there has not been a single full week of perfectly dry weather, and as a consequence the Cardiff Arms Park has beaten its miry record.

Saturday after Saturday the ground has been in a horribly heavy state, and as a result we have not seen the usual quantum of pretty football.

To-day's meeting of Cardiff and Newport on the Cardiff Arms Park was the fifth of the season, and it must at once be confessed that for the first time for a number of years the Usksiders have shown better and more consistent form than their near neighbours.

On that "fatal Thursday" in September Newport won at Uskside by 16 points to nil, but that this was false form was proved when Cardiff again went to Newport nine days later and played a drawn game. At Cardiff on November 30 Newport were again victorious by two tries to a dropped goal, but in that match Gwyn Nicholls was crocked early on, and was of little use to his side for the remainder of the game. Then came the remarkable combat on the Uskside ground three weeks ago, when Cardiff cracked Newport's record, after having rather the better of the luck. For to-day's final match of the season Cardiff were distinctly unfortunate in having no fewer than four of their international backs away through unavoidable causes.

So intense was the interest in this afternoon's game that three-quarters of an hour before the kick-off there were fully 5,000 spectators present, and this number had increased to 8,000 by three o'clock, half an hour before the time appointed for the start.

Cardiff's Weakened Side

Of course, the one topic of conversation all round the field were the prospects of the match. While it was admitted that Cardiff were heavily handicapped by the absence of so many of her clever backs, it was at the same time conceded that the recruits were all clever players, who were likely to strive their utmost to make a creditable show against their famous and brilliant opponents. Besides, when the Cardiff Club have perforce introduced young blood into their ranks they have always done well against Newport.

Yet it had to be recognised that Newport, with their full side out, are a great combination this season, and their backs are very difficult to stop. Then, on their left wing, they had two strong, fast, heavy, and experienced players like J. P. Jones and Melvile Baker opposed to two young recruits in Reardon and Ewan Davies, it having been decided to play R. A. Gibbs at left centre, with J. L. Williams as his wing.

The ground was in absolutely perfect condition for an attractive exhibition of Welsh Rugby football. It had dried so rapidly during the past couple of days that there was not a suspicion of softness left in the turf; yet it was springy, and the player receiving a heavy throw was not likely to be much hurt. However, from the river end the sun was shining brilliantly, and the side playing against it in either half was likely to be seriously handicapped. There was little or no wind blowing.

Besides the two changes at half and three-quarter in the Cardiff team, J. A. Brown was absent from the forwards, his place being taken by J. Groves, but Sergeant Fred Smith made a welcome re-appearance in the side. From the Newport team there was not a solitary absentee, unless the suspended player (R. Edwards) can be regarded as such.

An Enormous Crowd

As the time progressed the crowd increased enormously, and ten minutes before the start there were 25,000 people present. This number had increased to nearly 30,000 when the players lined up shortly after half-past three. The teams fielded in the following order:—

Cardiff: Back, R. Williams; three-quarter backs, J. L. Williams, Tom Evans, Ewan Davies, and R. A. Gibbs; half-backs, Reardon and C. Culverwell; forwards, F. Smith, J. Pugsley, W. Jenkins, J. Brookman, D. Pike, J. Casey, R. Jellings, and W. Groves.

Newport: Back, S. H. Williams; three-quarter backs, R. C. S. Plummer, J. P. Jones, F. W. Birt, and C. Perry; half-backs, T. H. Vile and W. J. Martin; forwards, C. M. Pritchard, E. Thomas, E. Jenkins, P. D. Waller, Dr. Smyth, H. Jarman, H. Uzzell, and P. Coldrick.

Referee: Mr. T. D. Schofield (Bridgend).

AN INTERESTING RECORD

	Cardiff.			Newport.		
	G.	T.	P.	G.	T.	P.
SEASON 1893-4.						
October 21, at Newport...	0	1	3	1	2	11
November 11, at Cardiff	1	1	8	0	1	3
January 13, at Newport	0	0	0	0	3	9
March 3, at Cardiff	2	0	10	0	0	0
SEASON 1894-5.						
October 20, at Cardiff...	0	0	0	0	0	0
November 26, at Newport	0	0	0	1	1	8
March 30, at Newport ...	0	1	3	1	0	5
April 10, at Cardiff.........	1	0	5	0	2	6
SEASON 1895-6.						
October 19, at Newport..	0	0	0	0	0	0
November 23, at Cardiff	0	2	6	1	0	5
February 15, at Newport	1	0	5	1	2	11
March 21, at Cardiff......	0	0	0	1	1	8
SEASON 1896-7.						
October 17, at Cardiff......	0	0	0	0	1	3
November 28, at Newport	0	0	0	2	2	16
February 13, at Cardiff..	0	2	6	3	0	13
March 11, at Newport...	0	1	3	0	0	0
SEASON 1897-8.						
October 23, at Newport...	3	2	21	0	1	3
November 27, at Cardiff	0	1	3	0	0	0
February 26, at Newport	1	5	20	1	2	9
March 26, at Cardiff.....	3	1	18	0	0	0
SEASON 1898-9.						
October 22, at Cardiff......	1	1	8	0	1	3
November 29, at Newport	0	3	9	0	0	0
February 25, at Cardiff..	1	1	8	1	0	5
March 25, at Newport.	1	0	5	2	0	9
SEASON 1899-1900.						
October 21, at Newport..	1	0	5	2	1	13
November 24, at Cardiff	1	0	4	0	1	3
February 24 at Newport	0	0	0	0	2	6
March 24, at Cardiff	0	3	9	0	0	0
SEASON 1900-1.						
October 20, at Cardiff...	0	2	6	2	1	12
November 24, at Newport	0	2	6	3	0	15
February 23, at Cardiff..	1	0	3	1	1	8
March 23, at Newport ...	2	0	10	0	0	0
SEASON 1901-2.						
October 19, at Newport..	1	1	7	0	1	[illegible]
November 23, at Cardiff	1	1	7	1	0	5
February 22, at Newport	0	2	6	1	0	4
March 22, at Cardiff......	0	0	0	1	2	10
SEASON 1902-3.						
October 18, at Cardiff....	0	0	0	0	1	3
November 22, at Newport	0	0	0	0	1	3
February 21, at Cardiff	0	0	0	0	0	0
March 21, at Newport.	1	0	5	4	3	28
SEASON 1903-4.						
October 17, at Newport..	0	0	0	1	0	4
November 21, at Cardiff	2	1	9	0	1	3
February 20, at Newport	0	1	3	0	1	3
March 19, at Cardiff......	0	1	3	0	1	3
SEASON 1904-5.						
October 15, at Cardiff...	2	1	11	0	1	3
Nov. 19, at Newport......	1	0	5	1	1	7
February 18, at Cardiff.	3	2	21	0	0	0
March 18, at Newport...	0	1	3	0	2	6
SEASON 1905-6.						
Oct. 14, at Newport...	3	1	17	0	1	3
Nov. 18, at Cardiff...	1	3	14	0	2	6
Feb. 17, at Newport.	1	2	10	0	1	3
Mar 17, at Cardiff ...	4	1	20	1	0	5
SEASON 1906-7.						
Oct. 13, at Cardiff ...	0	1	3	0	0	0
Nov. 17, at Newport.	1	2	11	0	0	0
Feb. 16, at Cardiff ...	1	0	3	0	1	3
Mar. 16, at Newport.	0	0	0	0	0	0
SEASON 1907-8.						
Oct. 12, at Newport.	1	1	7	1	0	3
Nov 16, at Cardiff.	0	2	6	0	1	3
Feb. 15, at Newport.	0	2	6	0	1	3
Mar. 7, at Cardiff.	0	1	3	0	1	3
SEASON 1908-9.						
Oct. 10, at Cardiff ...	3	0	15	1	1	8
Nov. 14, at Newport	2	1	11	1	0	5
Feb. 13, at Cardiff ...	2	1	12	1	2	11
Mar. 18, at Newport	Abandoned, snow.					
SEASON 1909-10.						
*Sep. 30, Newport ...	0	0	0	2	2	16
Oct. 9, at Newport ..	1	0	4	1	0	4
Nov. 13, Cardiff	1	0	4	0	2	6
Feb. 12, Newport	0	3	9	1	1	8

* Instead of match abandoned in March, 1909.

The Game

Newport won the toss, and elected to play against the sun in the first half. It was noticed that, after all, R. A. Gibbs was playing right centre, with Ewan Davies on his wing. Cardiff had the better of the opening play, and the game settled on the Newport 25 line, where Culverwell was soon penalised for putting the ball in unfairly, Newport gaining 25 yards from the kick. Newport were next penalised for "feet up," and Cardiff gained a slice of ground. From a scrum at the centre the Cardiff forwards broke away, with Casey and Brookman in the van, and they were not stopped until Stanley Williams pulled them up in his own 25. Here Reardon missed a good pass from Culverwell, but the Cardiff forwards continued to do well, and at this stage were more than holding their own.

Culverwell, Reardon, and J. L. Williams passed very smartly, and the defence was almost beaten. Very strenuously play was fought out in the Newport 25, but Vile gained half the length of the field with an enormous kick to touch.

Culverwell was penalised for palpable offside, and Burt took a long shot at goal, the ball going wide and Tom Evans touching down.

A Keen Game

saving his own life.

It was a keen and splendidly-fought game, with Cardiff having slightly the better of it up to date. Newport were penalised by the referee, and Gibbs gained a lot of ground with a long kick. Tom Evans took a good pass from Culverwell and kicked to touch at the Newport 25. Evans was again prominent with smart play, and there was a promising movement, but Reardon threw a wild pass. Vile was penalised, but Gibbs had his shot for goal charged down, and was himself injured at the same time.

Cardiff got the ball from most of the scrums, but Burt put his side on the attack with a great kick to touch. Newport passed grandly, and seeme dto have the defence well beaten, when J. P. Jones passed to Baker, but Reardon rushed the wing man into touch-in-goal with a wonderful tackle.

Uzzel Injured

Newport at this point were a man short, Uzzel having to retire to the touch-line with an injury.

Good kicking by the Cardiff backs enabled the home team to again get on the aggressive, and Casey and Jellings showed good form at the line-out. The game continued in the Newport half, and Uzzel came back to play. The visiting pack were not showing the form expected of them, and, if anything, were outplayed by the home eight. Most of the passing accomplished up to this point was done by Cardiff. Culverwell was doing very well at inside half, but Reardon, the outside man, was not sure in taking his passes. At halfway the Newport forwards were penalised for feet up, and Gibbs found touch 20 yards from the line. Much of the ground was recovered by Newport through a penalty against Culverwell for putting the ball into the scrum unfairly. The Cardiff forwards were going away admirably, when they were speedily pulled up by Vile, who effected a glorious save. Cardiff were having much the best of the game, but, although numerous efforts were made, their backs were unable to get properly into action.

Half-time:	G.	T.	Pts.
Cardiff	0	0	0
Newport	0	0	0

Rather a longe rinterval than usual was taken, the players having become overheated from the effects of the sun. Play was resumed in the presence of fully 30,000 spectators. Cardiff now had the sun in their faces, and could be pardoned if they did not do quite as well as in the first half.

Charlie Pritchard re-started for Newport, and the ball failing to reach the ten yards line, a scrum was ordered at the centre. Culverwell threw out a long pass to Ewan Davies, whic hthe recruit missed, but Gibbs was at hand to save nicely. Plummer saved a strong rush by the Cardiff forwards by gathering cleverly and kicking to touch. In a short rush by the home pack Culverwell and Vile were both kicked by a Cardiff for-

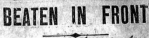

BEATEN IN FRONT

1909-10

Cardiff's Narrow Win

'CESTRIANS' GOOD FIGHT

Home Backs' Few Chances

CLEM LEWIS DOES WELL

By "PENDRAGON."

Final score:	G.	T.	P'ts.
Cardiff	1	2	11
Gloucester	1	1	8

Cardiff played their return fixture of the season with Gloucester on the Cardiff Arms Park this afternoon. On October 23 last, at Gloucester, the Welsh Metropolitans scored one of their best victories of the season, when they defeated the 'Cestrians by 20 points to 8. Cardiff played clever football that day, and quite merited their great success.

For to-day's game brilliant weather prevailed, but the ground was rather hard from the effects of the sun. There were important changes in the Cardiff team. T. Reardon played for L. M. Dyke at left centre, and the half-backs were C. Culverwell and Clem. Lewis. From the front rank F. W. Smith and J. Brown were absent, and their places were filled by J. Daley and the veteran Jack Powell, whom it was a pleasure to see back in the team.

The most notable absentees from the Gloucester team were Hudson and Vance. The players lined up in the following order:—

Gloucester: Back, W. Egerton; three-quarters, backs, T. Burns, W. Hall, E. Hall, and W. Washbourn; half-backs, J. Stephens and W. Dix; forwards, W. Jonns, H. Berry, D. Hollands, W. Pearce, N. Hayes, F. Pegler, and G. Holford.

Cardiff: Back, R. Williams; three-quarter backs, J. L. Williams, T. Reardon, W. Spiller, and R. Gibbs; half-backs, Culverwell and Clem Lewis; forwards, J. Pugsley, R. C. Jellings, W. Jenkins, J. Brookman, J. Groves, J. Pulman (Neath), J. F. Casey, and J. Powell.

THE GAME.

Cardiff made a sensational start, for Spiller deceived the defence by pretending to kick to the right, and then doubling to the left. He ran across and put in a long kick, the ball rolling very awkwardly for Egerton, who failed to field it until he was right on his own line. He was then promptly tackled by Reardon, and as a consequence he lost the ball, and Pugsley immediately snapped it up and dropped over the line for a try within a minute of the start. R. A. Gibbs failed to convert. Gloucester made two or three nice bouts of passing after this, but their handling work lacked finish. However, they kept Cardiff rather severely on the defensive. On the whole, the play was of a poor quality, and the home forwards were unable to give their backs many chances. Getting a pass from Culverwell, Clem Lewis made one very pretty opening on the grand stand side, and with a little bit of luck would have got clear up to the full-back, with J. L. Williams in attendance. W. Hall, the Gloucester right centre, made a really clever effort, in which he beat a number of Cardiff men, but was eventually held in the home 25.

A DELIGHTFUL TRY.

Gibbs and Spiller, with a dribble and follow up, reached the Gloucester half, and here Gibbs received from Culverwell. There followed a very pretty and effective round of passing, in which the Cardiff threes proved much too fast and skilful for the opposing four. Gibbs passed to Spiller, and he to Reardon. The latter ran up to Egerton, where he gave a perfect pass to J. L. Williams, and the latter ran over nicely with a delightful try. From a fairly easy position R. A. Gibbs just failed to convert.

Gloucester made a determined effort after this, and after smart handling Washbourne got away on the left, but was grandly tackled three yards from the line by Bobby Williams. The Gloucester full-back was playing poorly, and several times the Cardiff forwards had him in serious difficulties. Clem Lewis and Gibbs put in pretty play on the right wing, and Gibbs gave a long pass inwards to Brookman, who nearly got over. There was some exciting play on the Gloucester line, but the Cardiff men were erratic, and eventually Gloucester relieved to the centre, where the game was being waged at the interval.

Half-time:	G.	T.	Pts.
Cardiff		2	6
Gloucester	0	0	0

SECOND HALF.

Gloucester started the second half in good style, and a sharp attack enabled them to reach the Cardiff 25. The 'Cestrians now had the bright sun in their eyes, and it was likely to bother them considerably. Vears broke away fine ly for Gloucester, and dashing right through the backs, he seemed likely to score, when Bobby Williams brought him down with a glorious tackle in front of the posts. However, a moment later the visitors rushed over, and Pegler scored. Egerton failed with the goal kick, which was almost a straight shot.

At the centre Gibbs went away with a dribble, and took the ball right over the line behind the posts for Jellings to score. Gibbs converted. In the visitors' 25 Jack Powell did some good work in the line-out, once giving a very clever pass to Gibbs. Bobby Williams fielded the ball at the centre, right in front of four or five Gloucester forwards, and the instant he kicked the ball was bashed to the ground. The plucky Cardiff full-back was assisted off the ground with his face bleeding, but only to return in a few minutes, amid general cheering.

RAGGED PLAY.

From the centre Gibbs and Spiller ran, passed, and kicked to the visitors' line, where there was some hot play. In the furious work hereabouts, E. Hall was injured and had to be assisted into the ambulance room. He was subsequently taken off the field with a sprained back. Reardon made a burst through the centre and almost put J. L. Williams over. Gibbs received a long pass out, and made a fine run down the right wing, but passed inwards to Spiller when he seemed to have a good chance of beating the full-back on his own. Spiller, who took the pass, just failed to get there. The play was ragged, and neither side showed really good form. Cardiff attacked almost till the end of the game, but just before the finish Spiller was tackled, and lost the ball, with the consequence that W. Hall snapped it up, ran up to Bobby Williams, where he passed to Berry, who doubled inwards and ran over near the posts, Egerton converting.

Final score:	G.	T.	P'ts.
Cardiff	1	2	11
Gloucester	1	1	8

Comments.

It was not a really good game, but there were occasional exciting incidents. Cardiff's forwards were again beaten, and the home backs had few chances of showing their ability.

In open play the Cardiff front rankers did well, but for gaining possession in the scrimmage they were not to be compared with the Gloucester eight.

This was a pity, for by the quality of their second try it was evident that the home backs were in good form could they have got the ball as often as the opposing rear division.

On the general run of the play it was an equitable result; for Cardiff hardly deserved to win by more than three points, and yet they certainly showed the better class of football. Undoubtedly, apart from the heeling work of the forwards, they were all round the superior side, and it was really a pity that the backs could not get a greater share of the ball.

With their paucity of chances Culverwell and Clem Lewis performed very capably at half and when at times they seemed to compare unfavourably with the opposing couple it was because the latter were so much helped by their forwards.

Lewis has every appearance of being a coming man. He takes the ball well, can cut out an opening, is a good tackler, and is not afraid to go down to the ball. In short, while he lacks a great deal of Percy Bush's brilliance, he is also devoid of some of the defects of that famous player, and it is quite possible that he will fit in better with the passing machinery of the Cardiff team.

Culverwell has rendered invaluable service to Cardiff during W. L. Morgan's incapacity, and to-day again he was quite a success.

Spiller and Gibbs were the best of the threes. J L. Williams had few chances. Reardon performed better in the centre than he has done in other positions, and took his passes more safely than he has been accustomed to do. He will yet make a name for himself.

Bobby Williams gave one of his best displays at back, and everybody was sorry to see him knocked out. It is really questionable whether a player is justified in attempting to kick the ball in the position in which Williams was, for the Gloucester forwards were within a yard of him, and it was almost certain that he would be charged furiously. But there, Bobby Williams is Bobby Williams—the pluckiest player we have seen in Wales for years. He showed his pluck in returning to the field in a minute or two after his nasty injury.

Pugsley, Brookman, Jenkins, and Casey were the best of the Cardiff pack, and Johns, Berry, Vears, and Hollands were the most prominent of the visiting eight, who were more than a useful octette.

Although the Gloucester backs had the ball so often, they failed to make produtive use of it. Their passing was very plain, and easily anticipated. Stephens and the Brothers Hall were the best of their rear division.

CARDIFF AND GLOUCESTER AT CARDIFF.

A TUSSLE NEAR THE GLOUCESTER GOAL LINE.

A CARDIFF HALF ABOUT TO CLEAR.

...erting left Cardiff's margin but three points, and the final immediately came.

FINAL—	G.	T.	P.
CARDIFF.......................	1	2	11
GLOUCESTER...............	1	1	8

"Old Stager's" Remarks.

Though the excitement especially of the Barbarians and the close play in the Leicester match were missing, it was still a good game. The forward play reached a high standard, the visitors playing their usual clever and stolid style. Johns excellently led them, but Berry, Vears and Holford were generally in the van.

For Cardiff Jack Powell's return was hailed with satisfaction, and there was no one who approached indifference, while Brookman, Jenkins and Pugsley were most prominent. Pullman played a capital game, but he was handicapped by the rather different tactics of the home team as compared with Neath, who do more rushing.

It was a big battle at half. Dix, the recruit, is no mean scrum worker, but Culverwell was clearly his master. Clem Lewis made more friends and it will be a pity if his services cannot be retained for the club. He was seldom unable to part with the ball with advantage, despite the close attention paid to him, and took his fair share in the tackling.

Gibbs was the most prominent of the home three-quarters, and E. Hall the best of the visitors until his accident. The game was not distinguished by any brilliant incident, but the play on the whole reached the average standard.

These pages from Culverwell's collection show Cardiff's games with another great rival, Gloucester. The clubs had played each other regularly since 1882. There is again an impression of large crowds; Culverwell has identified himself by marking in an 'X'.

Another player from St Fagans was Billy Spiller, club captain in 1912/13. He was known to be very keen on his team's appearance and would have presumably been well-pleased with their neatness in this team line-up, which also shows the pavilion in all its splendour.

W.J. Jenkins, captain in the 1913/14 season, played 158 times for Cardiff between 1909 and 1920 and was capped 4 times by Wales. A fine forward, he would almost certainly have made more appearances for his country had war not intervened. He also served on the club committee.

The new South Grandstand was built during the summer of 1912 and could accommodate 3,000 spectators. At the same time, improvements to the North, East and West terraces provided room for another 40,000 fans. The total cost of the building work was £8,000. Although actually paid for – with £2,150 on deposit with Lloyds Bank and £2,500 from the Welsh Rugby Union, with the committee guaranteeing the rest of the money – the development was still an act of faith. The previous season had seen gate receipts drop, there had been coal and railway strikes and some supporters were going to watch Cardiff City at Ninian Park instead, with the result that there was an overall deficit of £214 14s 8d.

Action from the Cardiff v. Neath match of 1912 gives a good impression of the facilities on the East Terrace, including the distinctive scoreboard.

The ground improvements were opened on the occasion of the match against Newport on 5 October 1912. The splendidly named Lord Ninian Crichton Stuart, MP for Cardiff, kicked-off in front of a crowd of 25,000. A single dropped goal won the match for Newport. In fact, Cardiff won only five times in twenty-one games against their old rivals between 1909 and the outbreak of the First World War.

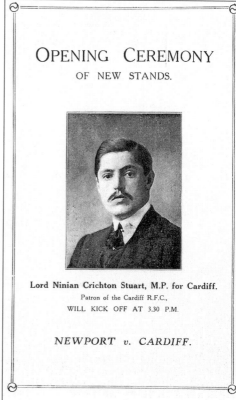

One of Cardiff's greatest forwards of the 1900s – and also one of its most interesting characters – was Billy O'Neill. The Cardiff RFC Museum and also several reference books refer to him as 'W. Neill' (the name he was commonly known by after his decision to drop the 'O' from his surname). He thought that being known as 'Neill' rather than his Irish family name would increase his chances of being selected for Wales! As it was, he was chosen on merit and won 11 caps for the Welsh XVs that won the Triple Crown in 1905 and the Grand Slam in 1908. He was a great servant for the Cardiff club, playing 204 games in over a decade from 1898, before sheer economic necessity took him to the North of England to play rugby league for Warrington.

Three of 'W. Neill's' caps – for Glamorgan, the 1903 WRU Final Trial and Wales – are in the club museum, but his Wales Northern Union cap is in Moscow, where his daughter now lives. Billy returned to Cardiff in the spring of 1910, having played 55 games for Warrington and twice for Wales. He died in 1955.

The exploits of the Cardiff team even attracted the attention of the world of art (see opposite page). In 1912 and 1913, the French Cubist Robert Delauney painted three versions of 'L'Equipe de Cardiff'. The club had played Stade Francais at the Parc des Princes in February 1912. The Western Mail reported that the match had started 'at the unusually late hour of four o'clock in order to give the Parisians enjoying the Shrove Tuesday half-holiday an opportunity to attend the game...There was an enormous concourse of spectators'. Cardiff won 19-3 and, several months later, Delaunay painted the first of his three versions and exhibited it in Berlin. All three were based on a newspaper clipping (shown above) of a rugby match. There was some artistic licence with the colours of the jerseys and the addition of motifs such as the Eiffel Tower and the Ferris Wheel. The second and third versions are now in Eindhoven and the Musee d'Art Moderne in Paris.

Above Left: George Dobson was a coal-trimmer from Pontypridd and a stalwart in the Cardiff pack in 106 games between 1893 and 1901, often alongside his brother Tom. He played once for Wales in the 12-3 defeat of Scotland at Swansea in 1900. Tragically, George did not enjoy good health and, after several illnesses, died at the age of forty-four.

Above Right: Jim Casey joined Cardiff from Pill Harriers in September 1906 and played with Billy O'Neill in the Cardiff pack of seven forwards that took on the Springbok 'eight' on New Year's Day 1907 and secured a famous club victory, winning 17-0.

Joe Pugsley was another tough-as-nails forward from the Cardiff docks. He was a member of the Cardiff XV that beat the Wallabies in 1908 and won 7 Welsh caps before joining Salford Rugby League Club in 1911. He died at the age of ninety-one in 1976.

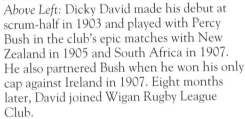

Above Left: Dicky David made his debut at scrum-half in 1903 and played with Percy Bush in the club's epic matches with New Zealand in 1905 and South Africa in 1907. He also partnered Bush when he won his only cap against Ireland in 1907. Eight months later, David joined Wigan Rugby League Club.

Above Right: William Llewellyn Morgan was the brother of Teddy Morgan, who scored the try for Wales that beat the 1905 All Blacks. Like Dicky David, 'WL' Morgan was a one-cap wonder at scrum-half, but he also played in two tests for the Anglo-Welsh team that toured New Zealand in 1908. He played 75 times for Cardiff between 1905 and 1912.

Louis Dyke captained Cardiff in 1911/12. He scored 33 tries in 107 games for the club and was capped 4 times in the centre for Wales. A product of Christ College, Brecon, he was a popular captain who also played for the Barbarians.

Above: Football Club Records was a series of 50 cigarette cards, marketed by F. & J. Smith in 1917. Amongst the major soccer clubs of the period is card no. 48, which gives the Cardiff Rugby record for 1913/14 and, on the other side, a portrait of Clem Lewis. The results are not complete with four matches, including the away fixture with Headingley, missing. One of the rare breed who played top-class rugby before and after the First World War, John Morris Clement Lewis played 229 games for Cardiff between 1909 and 1924 and was capped 11 times at fly-half for Wales between 1912 and 1923. He was club captain in 1920/21 and also captained Wales twice.

Left: With fourteen defeats in forty games, 1913/14 was by no means one of Cardiff's greatest seasons. However, in one of their final home games before the First World War, Headingley were beaten 14-6. Another excellent programme, which in 1914 had a full colour crest on the front cover and was folded to create eight pages, contained a team photograph and the season's results up to, and including, the previous afternoon's game against Harlequins. It was printed by the *Western Mail.*

Five
The Cost of War

The cost of war between 1914 and 1918 included the lives of gifted sportsmen such as John Lewis Williams and David Westacott. J.L. Williams was one of Wales' greatest wings, with 17 tries in 17 games, and he also played two tests in New Zealand for the Anglo-Welsh team of 1908. His 199 games for Cardiff included a season as captain in 1909/10. Serving as a captain in the Welch Regiment, he was killed at Mametz Wood during the Battle of the Somme on 12 July 1916 (he was thirty-four years of age). Dai Westacott , a native of the Grangetown area, played 120 times for Cardiff before his retirement in 1910. He was an uncompromising forward who played once for Wales against Ireland in Belfast in 1906. During the war, he was a private in the Gloucestershire Regiment and was killed in action in France on 28 August 1917 at thirty-five years of age.

The outbreak of war in August 1914 brought a halt to official fixtures involving Cardiff Rugby Football Club for five years (unofficial fixtures would resume in 1918). During the war years, Cardiff Arms Park became the venue for various recruitment and charity events. An open-air boxing tournament was held on 22 May 1915 and was well-attended by both military officers and leading civilians, who aimed not only to generate much-needed money to support the war effort but also to assist with further recruitment.

The tug-o'-war was part of a sports day, held on 17 August 1917, by which time money was needed to help the many wounded soldiers of the city.

Following the Armistice in November 1918, what became known as the Cardiff Rugby (War Charity) Football Team played a series of matches that raised £1,942 for charity during the season. The secretary of the organising committee and also captain of the team – shown holding the ball – was Frank Gaccon. The chairman, seated far left, was R. Fitzgerald.

One innovation to encourage recruitment during the war and to help military charities was the introduction, in December 1917, of a ladies' match at the Arms Park. This Cardiff team, which was beaten 6-0 by Newport Ladies, were for the most part employees of Hancocks Brewery. The Cardiff captain was Miss E. Kirton, an employee of the Grand Hotel in Westgate Street where the teams changed. 'Ma' Rosser, who is said to have 'greatly assisted the cause of rugby football in Cardiff', is included in the picture.

As organised representative rugby slowly re-emerged in the spring of 1919, a series of inter-services matches were played in Britain and France. One participant was Cardiff's Wickham J. Powell, a speedy wing who was to be capped in 1920. This diploma of honour from the French War Ministry was presented to him for captaining a Welsh XV in Paris in 1919.

Wick Powell's demobilization certificate tells us that he enlisted on 29 October 1914, that he did not serve overseas, and that he was discharged on 14 December 1918.

Six
Years of Ambition

Cardiff first played the Barbarians in March 1891 and between 1900 and 1920 played them twice a season, at Christmas and Easter. By 1927, however, the club had started a controversial two First XVs policy for every Saturday, which divided their playing resources. Even so, for a match like this on Easter Saturday in 1927, the Cardiff team still featured the likes of Ossie Male, Harry Bowcott, Idris Richards and Bob Barrell and beat a Baa-Baas outfit including Dan Drysdale, Windsor Lewis and Herbert Waddell by the handsome score of 16-8.

Following his demobilisation from the Army, Wickham Powell took over as First XV captain midway through the 1919/20 season for the first official games after the war. A new generation of club players included the Cornish brothers, Arthur and Willie, Idris Richards, and the Irish internationals Finlay and Wallace.

Charley Bryant, Wickham Powell and Arthur Cornish were three of the club's most effective players during a difficult season, in which thirteen games were lost. Bryant had first played for the club in 1910 and was to lead the Reserve XV from 1921 to 1923. He won a pair of caps for Ireland in 1920. Cornish, one of four brothers to play for the club, gave noble service in 267 games over thirteen seasons, played 10 times for Wales and became an administrator for both club and country. Powell not only played for Wales throughout 1920 but also won the Powderhall Sprint. A period in rugby league was followed by a return to Cardiff, where he was the licensee or landlord of four pubs – including the nearby City Arms from where he retired in 1959.

Great social traditions are never far from the surface at the Arms Park. In the 1920s, it was a case of kippers in the pavilion after training. Here, pre-war players Dan Callan and Anthony Baker (in the background) are seen with, amongst others, Jack Powell and 'Codger' Johnson (front right).

Thomas Johnson, known as 'Codger', was a schoolboy international who joined Cardiff after a season with Penarth. He was a powerful runner who made 187 appearances for the club (see page 92).

Jim Sullivan appeared only briefly for Cardiff Rugby Football Club – but he may have been the greatest rugby player ever produced by the city. The records show that he scored only a single try in 38 games for the club, but there was much more to Sullivan than that. Born in the city on 2 December 1903 and educated at St Albans School, he made his first team debut against Neath on 16 October 1920 – in other words, at the age of sixteen years and ten months. Two months later, this boy wonder of a full-back played for the Barbarians against Newport. Then, after starring in the Welsh international trial, young Jim was put on standby for the Wales XV to play France on 26 February 1921. If he had played, he would have been capped at seventeen years old. Jim Sullivan was an apprentice boilermaker in Cardiff and times were hard, so it was no surprise when he went north to Wigan for a record signing-on fee of £750 – matching the sum paid the previous year to Wickham Powell. It was in rugby league that he became an all-time great. He was to play 922 games for Wigan and score over 6,000 points before retiring in 1946 at the age of forty-three, having appeared in a world record 60 tests. He was almost certainly the greatest rugby player, union or league, of the inter-war years. Jim Sullivan died in September 1977.

Jim Sullivan shaking hands with Max Rousie before the France *v.* Wales rugby league international of 1936.

A fine image of Jim Sullivan in rugby league action.

Above: When international rugby returned to Cardiff Arms Park after the First World War, the first match was against Ireland. Cardiff's only representative in the Wales team was Wickham Powell – but the club provided two of the Irish XV.

Above Right: Dr Tom Wallace was a GP in the city and played 155 games for the club between 1919 and 1925. He was also captain in 1922/23. Later, he served on the committee and became the club's medical officer.

Below Right: Dr James Finlay won Irish caps both before and after the war and appeared briefly for the club in 1919/20. To complete a unique treble, Charley Bryant also played for Ireland in 1920 but missed the game against Wales.

GATES OPEN AT 1 P.M.   KICK OFF AT 3.30.

NAMES OF PLAYERS AND POSITIONS

Referee : Mr. Potter Irwin, English Rugby Union

IRELAND.	WALES.
Full Back.	**Full Back.**
1 W. CRAWFORD, Lansdowne	1 JOE REES, Swansea.
Threequarters.	**Threequarters.**
2 J. A. DICKSON, Dublin Univ. (Right Wing)	2 WICK POWELL, Cardiff (Right Wing)
3 W. DUGGAN, Univ. Coll., Cork (R. Centre)	3 J. P. JONES, Pontypool (Right Centre)
4 T. WALLACE, Cardiff (Left Centre)	4 ALBERT JENKINS, Llanelly (Left Centre)
5 P. McFARLAND, Derry (Left Wing)	5 BRYN WILLIAMS, Llanelly (Left Wing)
Half Backs.	**Half-Backs.**
6 A. K. HORAN, B'heath (Inside)	6 T. REEVES, Cross Keys (Inside)
7 W. CUNNINGHAM, L'downe (Out)	7 J. WETTER, Newport (Outside)
Forwards.	**Forwards.**
8 A. COURTNEY, Dublin University	8 H. UZZEL, Newport (Captain)
9 R. CRIGHTON, Dublin University	9 T. PARKER, Swansea
10 W. D. DOHERTY, Guy's Hospital	10 EDGAR MORGAN, Llanelly
11 J. FINLAY, Cardiff	11 J. WILLIAMS, Blaina
12 W. J. ROCHE, University College, Cork	12 S. MORRIS, Cross Keys
13 P. STOKES, Garryowen	13 R. HUXTABLE, Swansea
14 N. POTTERTON, Dublin Wanderers	14 J. WHITFIELD, Newport.
15 H. COULTER, Queen's Univ. Belfast	15 G. OLIVER, Pontypool

THE ROATH FURNISHING CO. BRANCHES EVERYWHERE

The team page from the first post-war international programme in Cardiff. A crowd of 35,000 saw Wales score 6 tries and win 28-4. Though not shown in the programme, Tom Wallace captained Ireland.

The 1924/25 team was captained by 'Codger' Johnson, a wing or full-back who played 12 times for Wales. Thomas Albert, to give him his real names, attended school in Cardiff Docks, where he later worked as a ship's chandler. As a captain he led by example, becoming the top try-scorer with 25 in a season in which the team was beaten in eleven games.

Left: Arthur Cornish was one of the stars of Johnson's team, despite a minor disagreement that caused him to leave the club for a short while at the start of the season. He returned to play against the All Blacks. An all-rounder both on and off the field, Cornish played soccer for Cardiff Corinthians, rugby 10 times for Wales, captained the club in 1922/23, and went on to become a distinguished administrator. As well as being chairman and secretary of the club in the 1940s, he was chairman of the Welsh selectors. Robert Arthur Cornish died in July 1948 at the age of fifty-one. *Right:* William James 'Bobby' Delahay was a great character of Welsh rugby in the 1920s. During his 18 games for Wales, he played at scrum-half, fly-half, and centre, but for Cardiff he mainly played at the base of the scrum. He was outstanding in the club's game against the 1924/25 All Blacks. A builder from Bridgend, Bobby played 148 games for the club and was captain in 1927/28 before playing the final eight years of his career in Torquay. He eventually returned to Bridgend, where he died in 1978.

There was another titanic match with the All Blacks in 1924. This was the great team, captained by Cliff Porter, that has gone down in rugby history as 'The Invincibles', with the enviable record of played thirty-two, won thirty-two. They had players like George Nepia, Mark Nicholls and the Brownlie brothers, and 40,000 saw Cardiff hold their own in a match in which there was little back play. Eventually the tourists won 16-8; a week later they overwhelmed Wales by 19-0.

93

Two years later, another team from 'down-under' were playing at Cardiff Arms Park. The Maoris were less successful than their predecessors, losing seven matches on a seven-month tour. They played Cardiff twice. These are the teams in the first of those games on 6 November 1926. Cardiff were expected to win but foolishly threw the ball around in wet conditions. Things looked good at 8-8 at half-time, but the club's unforced errors gave the Maoris two tries after the interval for a clear 18-8 victory. The return match on 28 December was a much better game, watched by 22,000, with the visitors only just winning 5-3.

The Cardiff programme has always been a quality product and the team cameos in the Maoris' match souvenir are no exception. Ossie Male was reported to be 'Adept at all forms of puzzles, competitions, crosswords and the like. Sucks cider through a straw – yet of graceful build'.

In the same programme, we are told that Idris Richards 'Safeguards the interests of the Midland Bank at Pontypridd…is the team's infant and a man of influence and delightful company…a keen theatre-goer and dancer and an authority on international debts'. His namesake Gwyn, by the way, was described as 'The club's successor to Valentino. He has his own barber – note the exclusive style of haircut…' – not bad for an underground worker from Bryncethin!

A club cap for 1926/27, when there were two First XVs. This controversial experiment resulted in eighty-two games being played during the season – forty-seven by the 'A' First XV and thirty-five by the 'B' First XV. Between them they lost twenty-seven games, which pleased no one. The policy continued for all of five seasons, despite complaints as early as 1928/29 from clubs such as Leicester, Northampton and Aberavon that Cardiff were not fielding their strongest team against them. At the end of 1930/31, with the 'Other XV' using eighty players and winning only twelve out of thirty matches, the experiment was discontinued.

Trevor Lee, a Glamorgan policeman, did not play frequently for Cardiff before moving to Penarth, although his brother Fred had nearly 70 matches under his helmet, but the full-back managed a club record. On 8 September 1926, against Cardiff & District, he converted 12 tries and kicked a penalty – 13 goals out of 14 kicks with the missed attempt hitting a post.

Another variation on the two First XVs situation – a busy Easter in 1927. Having beaten the Barbarians on Easter Saturday (see p. 85), Cardiff went on to play another three games, on Easter Monday, Tuesday and Wednesday. They lost only the last game of the four-match sequence. The spectators certainly got their money's worth. Over the same long weekend, the 'Other' team played three away matches at Torquay, Exeter and Ebbw Vale.

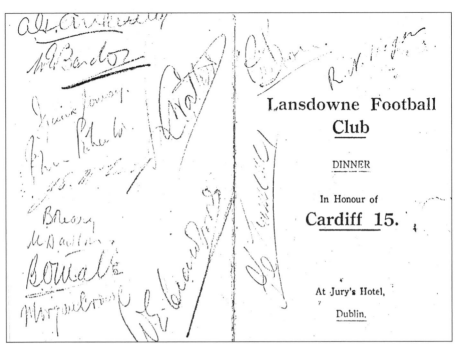

Lansdowne Football Club

DINNER

In Honour of

Cardiff 15.

At Jury's Hotel,

Dublin.

An interesting souvenir of the club's trip to Lansdowne in December 1928. Having already played London Irish on Boxing Day and then the Watsonians from Scotland the following day, Cardiff went to Dublin for a match, which they won 21-3, and a dinner they must have thoroughly enjoyed. Amongst the autographs is that of W.E. Crawford, a great full-back who played 30 games for Ireland and who went on to be President of the IRFU in 1957/58.

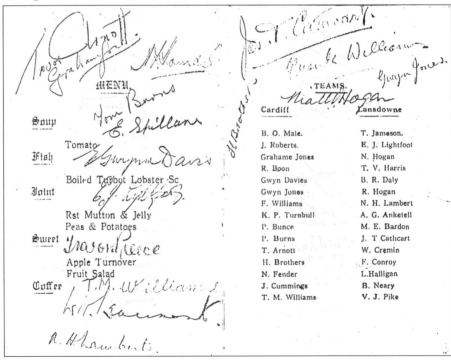

MENU

Soup

Tomato

Fish

Boiled Turbot Lobster Sc

Joint

Rst Mutton & Jelly
Peas & Potatoes

Sweet

Apple Turnover
Fruit Salad

Coffee

TEAMS.

Cardiff	Lansdowne
B. O. Male.	T. Jameson.
J. Roberts.	E. J. Lightfoot
Grahame Jones	N. Hogan
R. Bpon	T. V. Harris
Gwyn Davies	B. R. Daly
Gwyn Jones	R. Hogan
F. Williams	N. H. Lambert
K. P. Turnbull	A. G. Anketell
P. Bunce	M. E. Bardon
P. Burns	J. T Cathcart
T. Arnott	W. Cremin
H. Brothers	F. Conroy
N. Fender	L. Halligan
J. Cummings	B. Neary
T. M. Williams	V. J. Pike

Frank Williams was Cardiff born and bred but had a much travelled career in both South Wales (where he married Erith Maisie, the daughter of E. Gwyn Nicholls) and Yorkshire where he was sportsmaster at Queen Elizabeth Grammar School in Wakefield. He played 14 times for Wales. For the game against South Africa in 1931, when he partnered Claude Davey in the centre, the match programme listed him as Cardiff and Headingley and noted that his previous teams were Wales Schoolboys, Christ College, Brecon...and Cardiff Supporters! This is a useful reminder that in the 1930s the Cardiff Rugby Supporters Club did actually put a XV onto the field of play.

John Roberts scored 61 tries in 101 games for Cardiff and 5 tries in 13 games for Wales. Born in Liverpool and educated, like Frank Williams, at Cardiff High School, his later work as a Presbyterian minister took him to Northumberland and then Scotland. He was a much respected member of the club, first capped before his twenty-first birthday, who left the world of rugby behind him to go as a missionary to China at the age of twenty-five.

SOUVENIR PROGRAMME
OF
RUGBY MATCH

New South Wales
(The "WARATAHS")

VERSUS

Cardiff

Cardiff Arms Park, Cardiff
Saturday, December 3rd, 1927

Yet another of the successful overseas touring teams arrived in the autumn of 1927. Though the full Australia team have never beaten Cardiff, the New South Wales Waratahs secured a famous 15-9 victory, even though their top forward Jack Ford was sent off for dissent. In a bizarre scene, the Cardiff players pleaded for Ford to stay on, but to no avail. Referee Huntley reported Ford to the Welsh Rugby Union for 'disputing a decision'. What was beyond dispute was the Waratahs' victory by three tries to one, securing an historic double – the previous Saturday they had also beaten Wales at the Arms Park.

As always, a touring team match was celebrated in style. A five-course feast followed the game, at the nearby Grand Hotel in Westgate Street. As today, the Christmas season seemed to start early with mince pies and 'Xmas Pudding' proudly advertised amongst the sweet course.

Cardiff Athletic Club.
(FOOTBALL SECTION).

New South Wales
("WARATAHS")

v.

Cardiff.

Saturday, December 3rd, 1927

DINNER

GIVEN IN HONOUR OF THE VISIT OF THE NEW SOUTH WALES (WARATAHS) TOURING TEAM, TO BE HELD AT THE GRAND HOTEL, ON SATURDAY DECEMBER 3rd, 1927. at 6.30 p.m.

Journalism and communications of another age. Note that only a boy could be the Press Messenger, whose job it was to hotfoot it to the nearest telegraph office to send score updates to newspapers throughout the land.

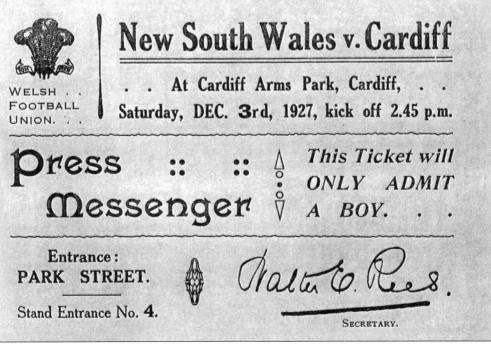

WELSH . .
FOOTBALL
UNION. . .

New South Wales v. Cardiff

. . At Cardiff Arms Park, Cardiff, . .
Saturday, DEC. 3rd, 1927, kick off 2.45 p.m.

Press :: :: Messenger

This Ticket will ONLY ADMIT A BOY. . .

Entrance:
PARK STREET.

Stand Entrance No. 4.

Walter E. Rees.

SECRETARY.

Two members of a great sporting family. Six Turnbulls played for Cardiff between 1923 and 1947. Bernard Ruel Turnbull won the most honours on the field, playing for Cambridge University, St Peter's, Cardiff, London Welsh, the Barbarians and 6 times for Wales. A hard-running centre, he was twice club captain and played 232 games over 10 seasons. He later became a trustee of the club and died in Hampshire in 1984, just a few months short of his eightieth birthday.

Maurice Joseph Lawson Turnbull, on the other hand, died young. He was killed in Normandy during the invasion of 1944, at the age of thirty-eight. He was arguably the most gifted games player of all: scoring 14,000 runs for Glamorgan, making 9 test appearances for England, playing international hockey and squash for Wales, as well as being the scrum-half in the first Welsh win at Twickenham in 1933. He was the only Welsh rugby international to play test cricket for England. However, he played only twice for Wales as injuries and cricket commitments curtailed his rugby career. As a batsman, he toured Australia, New Zealand and South Africa with the MCC and later became a test selector. Both on the field of play and as a Major in the Welsh Guards, Maurice Turnbull proved himself an exceptional leader of men.

Seven

The Pattern Established

CARDIFF RUGBY 1st XV FIXTURES. Season 1934-35.

Date	Opponents	Ground	Result	Date	Opponents	Ground	Result
1934				1935			
Sept. 1	Cardiff and District Rugby Union ..	Home		Jan. 1	Watsonians (Tour)	Away	
,, 8	Bristol	Home		,, 1	Penarth	Home	
,, 15	Neath	Home		,, 5	Llanelly	Away	
,, 22	Swansea	Away		,, 9	Bridgend	Away	
,, 29	Pontypool	Home		,, 12	Swansea	Home	
				,, 19	**England v. Wales** ..	Twcknm	
Oct. 6	Newport	Away		,, 26	Swansea	Away	
,, 13	Gloucester	Away		Feb. 2	**Scotland v. Wales**	Cardiff	
,, 20	Swansea	Home		,, 9	Gloucester	Home	
,, 27	Blackheath	Away		,, 16	Newport	Away	
				,, 23	London Welsh	Home	
Nov. 3	Llanelly	Away		Mar. 2	Newport	Home	
,, 10	Newport	Home		,, 9	Richmond	Home	
,, 17	Neath	Away		,, 9	**Ireland v. Wales** ..	Belfast	
,, 24	Plymouth Albion	Home		,, 16	Pontypool	Away	
				,, 23	Blackheath	Home	
Dec. 1	Coventry	Away		,, 30	Llanelly	Home	
,, 8	Llanelly	Home		April 6	Richmond	Away	
,, 15	Harlequins	Away		,, 13	Plymouth ..	Away	
,, 22	Bridgend	Home		,, 15	Falmouth } Tour	Away	
,, 26	London Irish	Home		,, 16	Penzance	Away	
,, 27	Watsonians	Home		,, 20	Barbarians	Home	
,, 29	Bristol .. .. } Tour	Away		,, 22	Harlequins	Home	
,, 31	Glasgow High School	Away		,, 23	Coventry	Home	
				,, 27	Penarth	Away	

CARDIFF ATHLETIC XV FIXTURES. Season 1934-5

Date	Opponents	Ground	Result	Date	Opponents	Ground	Result
1934				1935			
Sept. 1	Llanharan	Away		Jan. 5	**Final Trial**		
,, 8	Bristol United	Away		,, 12	Old Edwardians	Away	
,, 12	Chepstow	Away		,, 19	**England v. Wales** ..	Twcknhm	
,, 15	Tredegar	Away		,, 26	Pill Harriers	Home	
,, 22	Barnstaple	Home					
,, 29	Pill Harriers	Away		Feb. 2	**Scotland v. Wales**	Cardiff	
				,, 9	Gloucester United	Away	
Oct. 6	Newport United	Home		,, 16	Newport United	Home	
,, 13	Gloucester United	Home		,, 23		Away	
,, 20	Skewen	Away					
,, 27	Old Edwardians ..	Home		Mar. 2	Newport United	Away	
				,, 9		Away	
Nov. 3	Trial..			,, 16	Glamorgan Wanderers ..	Home	
,, 10	Newport United	Away		,, 23	Cardiff High School O.B...	Away	
,, 17	Cardiff H.S.O.B. ..	Home		,, 30	Pontyclun	Away	
,, 24	Maesteg	Away		April 6	Skewen	Home	
				,, 13	Chepstow	Home	
Dec. 1	Trial..			,, 20	Penygraig	Away	
,, 8		Away		,, 22	Farnstaple	Away	
,, 15	Maesteg	Home					
,, 22	Glamorgan Wanderers ..	Away					
,, 29	Bristol United	Home					

By the mid 1930s, with the disastrous two First XVs experiment long abandoned, Cardiff Rugby Club had established what was generally recognised as being the strongest fixture list of all clubs. There was an excellent balance of matches with the major clubs of England and Wales and attractive tours to Scotland over the New Year and the West Country in the Spring. However, sometimes there were disappointments. At Easter 1935, for instance, the club lost all three of their holiday fixtures for the first time.

Ronald Winston Boon has a special place in Welsh rugby history. Born and educated in Barry, he scored all the Welsh points – a dropped goal and a try – in the first Welsh win at Twickenham in 1933. He also scored a try for Cardiff against the 1931 Springboks. Ronnie Boon played 98 games for Cardiff over a ten-year period, up until the outbreak of the Second World War, and was also a great favourite at London Welsh and New Brighton. Like so many others of his era – Maurice Turnbull and Wilfred Wooller immediately spring to mind – Ronnie was a sporting all-rounder: he was a Welsh AAA sprint champion and also played cricket for Glamorgan. After a professional career in education that took him to Scotland, he returned to Barry to become president of the local rugby club and a town councillor. He emigrated to live with his daughter in New Zealand in 1995. He died there, in Waipukurah, in August 1998, at the age of eighty-nine.

The Cardiff team of 1931/32 was captained by Howard Poole, with Harry Bowcott as his vice-captain. Both went on the 1930 British Lions tour of New Zealand and Australia. Harry played in the centre in all four tests and Howard, who never got a Welsh cap, played at scrum-half against New Zealand in the third test at Auckland. However, 1931/32 was not a successful season on the playing field for the club: twenty games were lost and the captaincy was passed in mid-season to Harry Bowcott. On a happier note, the first ever Cardiff Athletic Club annual report was published at the end of the season. Its appearance every year was to be an invaluable record of all sporting and social achievements within the club.

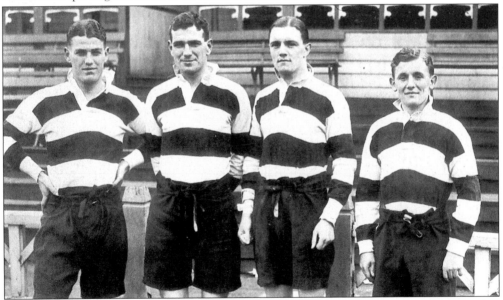

A happy photograph that shows the brothers Bowcott and Roberts. Harry Bowcott was another member of the Wales XV that won at Twickenham in 1933 and became a truly great administrator in the 1960s and '70s. His brother Jackie, a Cambridge Blue and impish scrum-half, partnered him for the club against the 1935 All Blacks. Though never capped, Jackie also partnered Cliff Jones in the 1933 Varsity Match at Twickenham. William Roberts was the younger brother of the missionary John and played with him against England in 1929. Bill and John opposed each other in two Varsity Matches.

Vol. XII. No. 12.

PRICE **2d.** EACH

CARDIFF RUGBY CLUB

❧ ❧ ❧

SOUVENIR
OFFICIAL PROGRAMME

❧ ❧ ❧

SOUTH AFRICA
(SPRINGBOKS)

v.

CARDIFF

CARDIFF ARMS PARK, CARDIFF
Saturday, November 21st, 1931

CARDIFF ARMS PARK, CARDIFF.
The historic ground of the Cardiff Rugby Club and venue of to-day's clash with the famous
" Springboks " of South Africa.

An interesting programme cover from 1931, showing the soon-to-be-developed Cardiff Arms Park. In a game watched by 34,000, Ronnie Boon got his try with a thrilling fifty-yard sprint, which beat his Springbok marker, but the tourists scored three tries of their own in a 13-5 win.

An imposing new North Stand was opened on 20 January 1934. The 380 ft long structure had 5,242 seats, while the floor of the stand gave covered accommodation for 8,750 and, in front, standing room for 9,100 (uncovered). Two seventy-six foot buffet counters ran the length of the stand in order, said a contemporary report, to enable spectators 'to secure refreshments in exactly the same way as is done at Twickenham'. Twenty-seven miles of timber, imported from Siberia, were used in the construction, along with bricks manufactured locally from material brought up from the Welsh mines. And the total cost? £20,000.

Artist Alan Brinkworth captures a moment during the building of the stand, with Cardiff scoring against Newport.

Where are they now? The main contractors, F.J. Thomas & Sons of Cardiff, were among the advertisers in special features to tell of the new stand but the names are now unfamiliar – though another advertisement shows that boxing was an expensive sport to follow, when compared with terrace tickets for the rugby international, at either 2s or 3s.

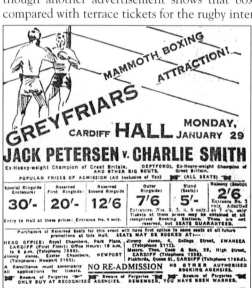

CARDIFF ARMS PARK—10.30 A.M. TO-DAY

JOHN BULL: Wonderful ground! Much more thrilling this afternoon, though, when the stands are up.

DAME WALES: Yes. John! But for the **real thrill** keep your eye on the score-board.

The cartoonist C.W. Nicholls, sadly for Wales, was wrong in his assessment as England won 9-0 and the Welsh selectors were severely criticised for choosing an inexperienced side. Nine of the team played their rugby outside Wales, five of whom became one-cap wonders and not a single one was currently representing Cardiff. Still, the new stand did help to bring up two new Welsh records: an attendance of 50,000 and gate receipts of £9,000.

Clean, Robust Rugby But Little Back Play

By "OLD STAGER"

	G.	T.	PL.
Cardiff	0	0	0
Newport	0	0	0

Attendance, 10,000

Living in the past afforded greater pleasure than living in the present to the spectators at the Cardiff Arms Park on Saturday.

They had gathered to see the playing of the 200th match between Cardiff and Newport, and many of them can be pardoned if they concluded that with the passing of the years the game they knew as Rugby had been afflicted with senile decay.

As far as back play was concerned that was a justifiable conclusion. But it was only the spectators who could complain, for the players spent a delightful afternoon in playing clean and robust Rugby. Before play started 80-years-old Col. Clifford Phillips, of Newport, kicked off, and in doing so merely repeated the opening kick he delivered in the first match between Cardiff and Newport in 1874.

Jack Bassett.

NEWPORT'S STRENGTH

That Cardiff's plans for Saturday's game were upset by the withdrawal of Harry Bowcott and the absence of Arthur Bassett is probable, though it is problematical as to what effect their presence would have had upon the trend of events having regard to the fact that Travers, the Newport hooker, was able to give both Regan and Wright a lesson in that particular art.

That was where Newport's strength lay and the wonder was, under those circumstances, that Hawkins and Dunn should have failed to induce their centres to find more adequate employment for the speed of Hopkin and Knowles on the flanks. All of Newport's regular heeling, and all of the individual dashes of Dunn and Squire went for nought.

For a portion of that Cardiff's sound defensive measures were responsible. The remainder were frittered away through Newport having no commanding personality to bustle his way through.

One of the surprising features, having regard to Newport's predominance in the scrummages, was that Cardiff should have done the major share of the attacking. The two factors which accounted for that were that Cardiff's forwards took the lead at the lines-out and in the loose, while the presence of Tommy Stone at outside-half and Jack Bassett at full-back meant that Cardiff had almost a monopoly of lengthy touch-finding.

NOT A SUCCESS

As an outside-half, however, Stone was not a success. He was too much under the domination of Newport's wing forwards, especially Fear, for that, and one often wondered if Fear was not too often favoured with "flying starts," in his attacks upon Bowcott and Stone.

With Stone caught in possession with unusual frequency, his centres, Brown and Cross, were subdued for attacking work, and the best of the play came from the dashes of A. H. Jones and Reardon. The former, in particular, was simply bursting with eagerness for the limited chances which came to him, though young Hopkin never ceased to worry or cover him. Hopkin certainly appears to be a good wing in the making, for he was little behind A. H. Jones in a match in which the few honours in back play went to the wings and Jack Bassett.

It was a game of disappointments rather than brilliance, with Newport's forwards effectively checking Cardiff by the simple expedient of carrying the scrummages. Teams:—

Cardiff: J. Bassett; W. Reardon, D. Brown, C. Cross, A. H. Jones; J. E. Bowcott, T. Stone; I. Wright, J. Regan, J. D. Jones, V. R. Osmond, L. M. Spence, Dr. E. N. Rees, K. Street, E. Watkins.

Newport: W. G. Lezke; W. H. Hopkin, K. Squire, A. R. Gear, J. T. Knowles; J. Hawkins, J. H. Dunn; J. R. Evans, T. Rees, V. J. Law, J. C. Jerman, W. Travers, W. G. G. Williams, A. G. Fear, M. Chatwin.

Referee, Mr. J. W. Faull, Morriston.

Col. Clifford Phillips Invited to Kick-Off

Cardiff's 200th Game With Newport

By "OLD STAGER"

The Cardiff Rugby Club has promptly acquiesced in the suggestion made in Thursday's "South Wales Echo & Express" that Col. Clifford Phillips, of Newport, shall be invited to kick-off in the match between Cardiff and Newport at Cardiff Arms Park to-morrow—a match unique in the sense that it will be the first occasion on which two clubs have met in 200 games.

The suggestion that an invitation should be sent to Col. Phillips to join in the game came from an enthusiast who desires to remain anonymous and was dictated by the fact that Col. Phillips was the Newport captain and kicked-off in the first match between Cardiff and Newport on April 5, 1875.

Mr. W. T. Morgan, president of the Cardiff club, has authorised the making of the request to Col. Phillips, with the intimation that Cardiff will be honoured if he will accept. Cardiff are thus paying a tribute to a delightful sportsman and a member of a great sporting family.

Col. Clifford Phillips.

It is worth recalling again, too, that it was the Phillips family who introduced Rugby to Newport, for when William and Clifford Phillips were taken to town by their parents in 1874 they brought with them the first Rugby ball seen in Newport. That, however, was not the first Rugby ball to be used in Wales, for there were several clubs that had been in existence in Wales for a couple of years prior to that.

THE FIRST MATCH

Col. Phillips had played Rugby at Oxford prior to coming to Newport, and was present at the meeting in his father's brewery when the Newport Club was formed in September, 1874. The intention then was that the club should play Association, and it was the inability of the club to secure fixtures in that code that was responsible for its turning its attention to Rugby and securing its first fixture with what was then known as the Glamorgan Club, Cardiff.

That first match resulted in a draw. At that time only goals counted in Rugby, and although Cardiff scored a try and a touch-down to nil, Newport were not vanquished.

Col. Phillips was one of Newport's two backs in that game, and in a chat on Thursday he remarked:

"I believe I was made captain that day because I had previously played the strict Rugby game at Oxford and could drop-kick. Punting was not allowed. With the exception of Graves, a Manchester man who played for Cardiff, practically the whole of the players knew little or nothing about the Rugby rules. Cardiff were all over us, but everything that both sides did was disputed."

Col. Phillips wrote a report of the match for the "South Wales Weekly Telegraph" of April 9, 1875, and he therefore claims that he was the first writer of Rugby in Newport, if not in the whole of Wales.

By the way, the captain of the Cardiff Club in the first match referred to was T. S. Donaldson Selby, while the secretary of the club, who also played in the match, was S. Campbell Cory.

The 200th game with Newport on 5 October 1935 understandably attracted great interest. Colonel Clifford Phillips had captained the Usksiders in the first ever derby match in 1876 and now took the kick-off nearly a half-century later. Although 10,000 fans turned up, the game ended in a stalemate. In a typically acerbic match report, Old Stager referred to a 'game of disappointments rather than brilliance'.

No history of Cardiff Rugby Club could fail to mention one of its best known and loved characters. Miss B.C. Filer, famed throughout the rugby world as 'Babs', was appointed stewardess of the club in November 1930, while still in her teens, at the salary of £2 a week. Babs was to remain in the post until 1973. She had taken on the role when the first bar was adapted from a part of the gymnasium in the old pavilion, large enough to host after-match meals for the players and for a piano and a singsong. The bar moved to more spacious premises under the North Stand and Babs served the club throughout the difficult Second World War years, during which bombs and landmines fell on the Arms Park, to be in control when the new clubhouse opened in 1956. Babs made the club a welcoming place for rugby lovers round the world.

One of the earliest captains during Babs' reign over the clubhouse was Tom Lewis, who led the team for the 1932/33 season – albeit by default as Harry Bowcott had been elected to the post but left to take up a position in London before the start of the season, leaving Tom, as vice-captain, to step in. Tom was just one of a long line of policemen who have represented the club: three of them captained Cardiff before the Second World War (the other two being Billy Spiller and Archie Skym). Tom Lewis won 3 caps for Wales and made 260 appearances for Cardiff between 1923 and 1933.

Tradition never dies at Cardiff Rugby Club. Thirty years after the great season of 1905/06, Percy Bush was back in the city and honoured by his fellow players. The legendary club names of

Spiller and Fred Smith, Gibbs and Gabe, Pugsley and Dicky David are still much in evidence at this happiest of gatherings at the Grand Hotel.

CARDIFF RUGBY TEAM, 1935-36.
(All Names Left to Right).
Back Row—**C. Cross, K. Street, A. Skym, *E. Watkins, *Dr. Noel Rees, *A. H. Jones,
*A. Bassett, *Harry Rees.**
Seated—**W. Reardon, *J. Regan, *Tommy Stone** (*Captain*), **L. M. Spence** (*Vice-Captain*),
J. D. Jones.
In Front—**J. J. Davies** (*Left*), **J. E. Bowcott** (*Right*).
*Players chosen for to-day's Match, in addition to the six players appearing underneath.
Photo by A. & G. Taylor, Cardiff.

R. W. BOON.

H. M. BOWCOTT.

V. R. OSMOND.

R. BALE.

H. O. EDWARDS

GWYN WILLIAMS.

A page from the match programme for the visit of the All Blacks in 1935. The Bowcotts were at half-back, Tommy Stone at full-back, Boon and Arthur Bassett in the three-quarter line and Les Spence, Eddie Watkins and Gwyn Williams in the back row. Unfortunately, the men in black won the game comfortably, with a 20-5 scoreline.

Another image of Harry Bowcott. His game against the All Blacks was not the happiest, probably because of an early injury. He had returned to Cardiff, having captained London Welsh in 1934/35. It was his final season with the Blue and Blacks, for whom he played 113 games and scored 36 tries. Harry eventually retired to live in Wenvoe and, at the time of writing, is the oldest surviving Welsh international at the age of ninety-one.

Archie Skym was a police constable from West Wales who joined Cardiff in 1929 and played 212 games for the club, besides winning 20 caps for Wales. Essentially a prop forward, Archie played his last game for Wales in the back row against England in 1935.

(signatures) John Donovan Lord Mayor 1934-35

W T Morgan

R Manchester

Jack Manchester

Tom Stone

W Warbrick Ref.

VISIT OF THE

NEW ZEALAND RUGBY FOOTBALL TEAM, 1935.

Reception and Dinner

GIVEN BY

The Lord Mayor of Cardiff

(Alderman JOHN DONOVAN, C.B.E., J.P.).

ON BEHALF OF THE CITY COUNCIL

AT THE CITY HALL, CARDIFF,

SATURDAY, 26TH OCTOBER, 1935

Post-match dinners would always feature local dignitaries, such as the Lord Mayor of Cardiff. The two captains in 1935 were Jack Manchester and Tom Stone and they have both signed this menu card, as have the referee and the All Blacks' manager Vincent Meredith.

Pat Caughey scores the first All Blacks' try in 1935. Tom Stone had dropped Caughey's speculative kick ahead. Later in the game, Caughey made the second try for Neville Mitchell and then scored the third himself.

Cardiff RFC, 1935/36. From left to right, back row: C. Cross, I. Heatley, A. Skym, E. Watkins, Dr N. Rees, W. Reardon, D. Brown, H. Rees. Middle row: J. Regan, K. Street, T. Stone (captain), L.M. Spence, A. Bassett. Front row: A.H. Jones, J.E. Bowcott.

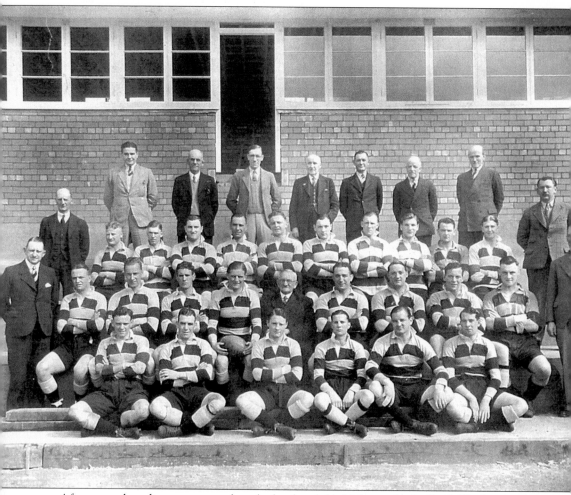

After several mediocre seasons of results by the club's high standards, Cardiff had quite a good season in 1936/37 and an even better one the following campaign. This squad of players, captained by Arthur H. Jones, finished 1937/38 with a record, including unofficial fixtures, of: played 51, won 43, drawn 2, lost 6. Jones had played twice for Wales in 1933, but then missed the best part of the next two seasons through serious illness. To everyone's delight he returned to the game and the club's annual report of May 1938 noted that Arthur Jones was 'a very capable and unselfish skipper...ever ready to encourage the selection of a younger or promising player, even if it meant standing down himself'. There are some notable faces amongst both committee and players in the photograph. At the back left is Hubert Johnson and two along from him is Danny Davies. The player on the left of the third row is Arthur Bassett and, next to him, a committeeman of the future, Gwyn Porter. Amongst the famous players in the middle row are Wilfred Wooller, W.E.N. Davies and Les Spence. The committeeman standing to the right of the players in the third row is the famous radio commentator, G.V. Wynne-Jones.

A player who captured the imagination of the Welsh rugby public as much as anyone in the 1930s was Cliff Jones. His 13 games as fly-half for Wales included the famous win over New Zealand in 1935. At various times he played for Cambridge University, Bridgend, Pontypool, Pontypridd and London Welsh. He scored 12 tries in 22 games for Cardiff, spread out over seven seasons up to the outbreak of the Second World War.

An unwanted claim to fame befell Cliff Jones on 1 September 1939. Returning to Cardiff after his legal studies, he dislocated an elbow in the first game of the season against Cardiff & District. Two days later, Britain declared war on Germany and official rugby came to an end for six years. One way or another, at the age of twenty-five, Cliff's glittering rugby career was halted. He was later to become the most respected of administrators, a Welsh selector for twenty-two years, and the President of the Welsh Rugby Union in the prestigious Centenary Season of 1980/81. Cliff Jones, a native of Porth, died in Bonvilston in 1990.

Henry Tudor (Harry) Rees was vice-captain to A.H. Jones in 1937/38, and won 5 caps in the Welsh pack – the first two in the second row and the rest at prop. He was a policeman from Pontypridd who played 169 games for Cardiff up to the outbreak of war in 1939. He died in Pentyrch in 1978.

Arthur Bassett was one of the most prolific try-scoring wings to play for the club. In just three full seasons, he scored 99 tries in 101 games before joining Barrow in January 1939. Curiously he failed to score for Wales in his 6 international appearances, but he had more luck up north. His trademark 'kick-and-chase', allied to an ability to run in tries from long distance, resulted in 64 touchdowns in 109 matches. Most spectacularly of all, on the 1946 Great Britain tour of Australia and New Zealand, he scored 18 tries in 11 games, including fewer less than 5 in the two tests he played against the Kangaroos.

D.E. Davies – a Blue and Black through and through. As a player, Danny Davies had 192 games, including the club captaincy in 1925/26, before his retirement in 1934. By then he was already a committeeman, as he was to be from 1927 until 1964. An inveterate keeper of records, he published the definitive statistical history of the club, notoriously sub-titled 'The Greatest', for the centenary in 1975. Danny fostered strong relationships with French rugby, particularly Stade Nantais and their secretary Henri Picherit. Outside the club, 'Massa Dan', a stickler for detail, was regarded highly enough to become honorary secretary of the 1955 Lions in South Africa and President of the Welsh Rugby Union in 1961/62.

Danny Davies scored 58 tries for Cardiff, including this effort against the Maoris in 1926.

Another great player and committeeman was Leslie Magnus Spence. Once described as 'tall, craggy, endearingly clumsy and awkward', he played 267 games, mostly at flank forward, in ten seasons up to the outbreak of war in 1939. Like Wilfred Wooller, he somehow survived the hardships of being a prisoner of war of Japan. On his release in 1945 he went on to become one of the club's longest serving committeemen over a period of forty years. At various times he was Chairman and President of the club and also President of the Welsh Rugby Union. Les Spence was, by common consent, one of the most able and popular characters ever to grace the club. At the time of his death in 1988 he was still President of Cardiff Athletic Club.

Two Athletic XVs captained by Hubert Johnson who, with D.E. Davies and Les Spence, completes a great triumvirate of Cardiff committeemen. Hubert captained the 'Rags' for three seasons from 1933, as well as making occasional appearances for the First XV. But it was as the supreme figurehead – and some would say lifeblood – of Cardiff Rugby Club that Hubert Johnson will always be remembered. During an association that lasted over fifty years, from the time he joined the club from Llandaff in 1927, he gave his undivided attention to the furtherance of rugby in general and the Cardiff Club in particular. He was known throughout the rugby world and for many was the public face of the club. He was President of Cardiff Athletic Club when he died in June 1979. It was soon decided to foster his memory by renaming the club's museum and, with due ceremony, on 16 December 1979 his great friend Les Spence officially opened The Hubert Johnson Room which, most appropriately, is 'Dedicated to rugby men throughout the world'.

One of Wales' greatest all-round sportsmen – some would say the greatest – was Wilfred Wooller. A native of Rhos-on-Sea and educated at Rydal School and Cambridge University, Wilf moved to live, work and play in Cardiff in 1936. For most of the next sixty years, he bestrode the sporting life of the city and South Wales like a Colossus. With three rugby and two cricket blues under his belt, not to mention a first cap for Wales as a twenty year-old in the first-ever win at Twickenham and a prominent role in the Welsh defeat of New Zealand in 1935, he was sure to leave his mark. A remarkably powerful young man, with his long strides and siege-gun kicking, he scored 30 dropped goals for the club (only Percy Bush has kicked more) as well as 38 tries in his 71 games. Wilf was captain of club and country in 1938/39 and was again leading Cardiff in September 1939 when the Second World War broke out. The war took a heavy toll on the young giant, who was incarcerated by the Japanese in Java for over two years. On his return to South Wales, cricket replaced rugby as his major sport. In a first-class career of 400 matches, he captained Glamorgan from 1947 to 1960, including the championship-winning season of 1948, and then became secretary for another seventeen years. An all-rounder in cricket – with over 13,000 runs, nearly 1,000 wickets and 400 catches – and an all-rounder in general with cricket, rugby, soccer, squash and, in later years, bowls all played in the most competitive spirit, Wilf was an undisputed leader of men. When Wilfred Wooller died in 1997, one obituarist called him 'the icon of a nation'. No one disagreed. The picture shows Wilfred Wooller in Cardiff's colours preparing for the game with England at Twickenham in 1937.

Above Left: A rare sight indeed as an injured Wooller is helped from the pitch.

Above Right: Wooller the rugby player was often depicted on cigarette cards. His first club was Sale and at various times he also played for The Army, London Welsh and the Barbarians.

Wooller the cricketer. His debut for Glamorgan was against Yorkshire at Cardiff Arms Park in 1938. He scored 1,000 runs in a season on four occasions and took 100 wickets twice. In 1955 he achieved the double of 1,000 runs and 100 wickets. He also played for Gentlemen *v.* Players and the MCC.

Official **PROGRAMME** **1939** **6ᴰ**

MIDDLESEX COUNTY R.F.U.

7

A-SIDE FINALS

THE SEVEN-A-SIDE MAN → ALWAYS PLAYING FOR CHARITY.

THAT IS WHY I AM PLEASED TO DRAW HIM WEARING THE NATIONAL FLAG.

GOOD FELLOW

TWICKENHAM
SATURDAY · APRIL 22 · at 1.30 ᴾᴹ

BY SPECIAL PERMISSION OF THE RUGBY FOOTBALL UNION

A successful day for player and club. In 1939 Cardiff played in the Middlesex Sevens and won the tournament at the first attempt. Wilfred Wooller took charge of the preparations – he had won there with Sale in 1936 – and was the victorious captain.

The winning Cardiff VII at Twickenham in 1939. The players are, from left to right, back row: Graham Hale, W.R. Davies, Evan Jones. Front row: Selby Davies, Gwyn Porter, Wilfred Wooller, Les Spence.

A reminder that the world was changing in 1940. Wilfred Wooller served with the 77th Heavy Anti-Aircraft Regiment and here he is seen as their captain

Afterword

Cardiff Rugby Club played its last official fixture for six years on 2 September 1939 when Bridgend were beaten 20-9 at the Arms Park. The next day Britain and Germany were at war. There would be hardship and devastation. At Cardiff Athletic Club, a War Emergency Committee was established and, whenever practical, unofficial wartime and charity matches were organised. An air raid on the city on 2 January 1941 left a landmine behind the goal-line at the river end of the Arms Park pitch and this further curtailed playing activities.

For the individual sportsmen of the city, promising careers were interrupted. Young men at the height of their powers like Wilfred Wooller and Les Spence went off to war and great personal suffering. A new generation of rugby stars would eventually replace them. At Cardiff Rugby Club, the youngsters who would be the sporting heroes of the future were already arriving.

Bleddyn Llewellyn Williams was not yet seventeen years old when war started. He had already played for the 'Rags' XV and would play for the RAF and Wales in the wartime games and would became the first post-war superstar in the decade that followed. As the sixty years' progress of the Cardiff club came almost to a halt in 1939, Bleddyn and several others like him were the hope for the future and would in years to come take the club onto even greater achievements. Their story is taken up in the second volume on the club.